THE
MEANING OF BEAUTY

THE
MEANING OF
BEAUTY

ERIC NEWTON

LONGMANS GREEN AND CO
LONDON   NEW YORK   TORONTO

LONGMANS, GREEN AND CO LTD
6 & 7 CLIFFORD STREET LONDON WI

ALSO AT MELBOURNE AND CAPE TOWN

LONGMANS, GREEN AND CO INC
55 FIFTH AVENUE NEW YORK 3

LONGMANS, GREEN AND CO
215 VICTORIA STREET TORONTO I

ORIENT LONGMANS LTD
BOMBAY CALCUTTA MADRAS

First published 1950
Reprinted - 1950

PRINTED AND BOUND IN GREAT BRITAIN BY
HAZELL WATSON AND VINEY LTD
AYLESBURY AND LONDON

CONTENTS

TO

DAVID OPPENHEIMER

WITHOUT WHOSE ACIDULATED COMMENTS
AT AN EARLY STAGE THIS BOOK
MIGHT HAVE TAKEN A
DIFFERENT DIRECTION

ILLUSTRATIONS

7

CHAPTER I

Introductory

I HAVE BEEN GOADED INTO WRITING THIS BOOK CHIEFLY BY THE doubts and hesitations that have always arisen in my own mind whenever I have found myself compelled to use the word 'beauty', but partly by the question, familiar enough in discussions on contemporary art, " Why have so many modern artists abandoned the search for beauty?" The double implication, that it is part of the artist's duty to search for beauty and that some contemporary artists of unquestioned reputation have failed to find it or have refused to look for it, seems to need a convincing answer. The stock answers— "The creation of beauty is *not* the artist's principal task" and "Our sense of beauty is so capable of development and expansion that it is dangerous to use the word as though it had an absolute value"—are far from satisfactory. The first provokes, in its turn, the reply that the creation of beauty may not be the artist's major preoccupation; but, none the less, artists are invariably judged by their power to create something that strikes the beholder as beautiful. The second leads to the further question, "But surely somewhere there is a yardstick? Here is a word for which there is no synonym, denoting a value that sooner or later becomes a major part of every human being's experience; do you tell me that it has, to all intents and purposes, no meaning?"

This book, then, is about the meaning of a word. It is certainly not a treatise on æsthetics. Except within the vaguest limits, beauty cannot be described: therefore it cannot be defined. It cannot be measured either in quantity or quality: therefore it cannot be made into the basis of a science. It has always proved impregnable to the frontal attacks of the æstheticians. None the less, it would seem reasonable to stalk the word, to outflank it and creep up on it from behind. Eventually one must have the courage to meet it face to face, but a preliminary

9

reconnaissance demands subtlety rather than courage. Beauty, let us say, is a recognisable quality; yet each person would draw up a different list of beautiful objects and give them different æsthetic indices. All that can be agreed upon is the nature of each man's reaction to his own list. In each case the sensation is not merely pleasurable, but pleasurable in the same way, and the sensation produced by objects at the top of the list is an intense one. A's list may be headed by the Sistine Madonna, while B's starts with the Blue Danube waltz—objects so dissimilar that no scientific method could possibly isolate, still less describe, the common factor which A and B would agree to call 'beauty'. And yet the sensations inspired by them have at least the common factors of pleasure and intensity. What kind of pleasure? And why so intense? Reasonable questions surely, yet the philosopher who attempts to answer them is playing a game of chess against desperate odds. Let him screw up his courage to move a single pawn, and he finds himself committed to a battle from which no one has yet emerged victorious. He is engaged—poor soul—in a struggle with his Creator, and his only weapons are words.

It is fascinating to watch the play of these doomed philosophers. Their usual method is that of the player who attempts to 'take' his opponent's Queen by substituting one of his own pieces for it. Words are his only substitutes. Here, in one corner, is Croce substituting for 'beauty' the word 'expression' or 'the expression of intuition'. There are the Freudians substituting 'wish fulfilment' or 'sublimation'. Kant and his followers think that 'play' is a serviceable pawn. Herder relies on 'empathy'. To enumerate all the known gambits would be boring. One need only consult a bibliography of æsthetics to realise what endless variations are possible. But one common factor emerges. They are all examining states of mind; they are not looking at beautiful things or listening to beautiful sounds. Their books are seldom illustrated. They are not analysing an inherent quality, but its effect on themselves.

There seems to be no valid reason for being more interested in an emotion than in its cause. I received recently a letter from a scientist in which the following sentence occurred—"One of the laws of thought ought to be, 'The way in which a phenomenon is manifested depends on the way in which it is observed' ".

This is so obviously true that it must be just as applicable to the atomic structure of matter or the speed of light as to the nature of beauty. What man calls 'colour', for example, is merely a sensation in the human eye caused by white light that has been interfered with in certain ways—usually by the molecular structure of the objects that reflect it. The nature of 'colour' depends on the construction of the eye. The word 'colour' can have no other meaning, but all one can do about it is to preface every attempt to describe a phenomenon by some such phrase as "within the limits of my own sensations and perceptions, and of the instruments at my disposal, I believe the following to be the truth". I am willing to admit these limitations, but I refuse on that account to believe that they cannot give me a serviceable account of the phenomenon perceived and examined.

It may be true, for instance, that the eyes of certain animals are better adapted to observe certain aspects of light than our own, and that one could imagine sensory organs which would react far more sensitively than our own to all kinds of wave-frequencies, which certainly exist and for which we have invented names, but of which we have no direct experience. But since we are ultimately concerned with the manner in which phenomena perceived by the human being produce in him certain emotional changes, it is useless to consider the phenomena that are unperceived and therefore produce no change. It is equally useless to remind ourselves that between reality itself and our limited consciousness of reality there is an enormous gulf. Since total reality is beyond our consciousness, we have not even a language that could express it. But what we can do is to deduce a universe from our experience of it. That is not quite the same thing as to describe our experience and then to mistake the description for a description of the thing experienced.

Consider for example that biggish group of philosophers gathered round St. Thomas Aquinas, and his disarmingly simple 'Id quod visum placet'. To say, "Whenever I see this I am pleased: therefore it must be beautiful" needs no massive intellect. To say no more than that is almost to refuse to make the first move in the game.

Or was St. Thomas, perhaps, unaware of the issue? Perhaps, in his day, that precious instrument for beauty-divining known as 'good taste' had not been invented. Perhaps he was not conscious that taste could be good or bad. If so, he was in a poor position for divining beauty. We of the twentieth century have built a kind of tower on the outskirts of the walled realm of beauty. Only by ascending that tower can one catch a glimpse of the delights within the wall. Free admission to the tower of good taste is, it seems, a prerogative of a handful of sensitive, educated people. But they, or some of them, are graciously willing to admit such of the outside world as will pay a few pence, read a few books and repeat the creed formulated for their benefit. From the top of the tower of good taste one can see a grand sweep of the surrounding country. And yet even from this vantage point the walls that encircle the domain of beauty always seem to be shifting. A map of these walls made in 1850 would be hardly recognisable as an indication of where they stand to-day. The Elgin Marbles, a bronze from Benin, a pitchpine dado, a picture by Albert Moore, a picture by el Greco, a church by Pugin, a factory by Gropius—are they inside or outside the wall? Were they always? Will they be a century hence? Would Sir Joshua and Ruskin and Roger Fry have admitted them all? Surely not. And surely it is somehow healthy for standards of beauty to shift this way and that. Evolution is at work. Would it not be a disaster if beauty could be reduced to a formula?

For the simpler, the more measurable things of life words are adequate. A man sees a rose or a mountain, he feels hot or hungry: at once it becomes necessary to invent the sounds 'rose', 'mountain', 'heat', 'hunger'. But a word, like a coin, should have the same value for everyone regardless of differences between the men who use it. A rose is a rose for us all, since botanists have decided on certain characteristics that belong to roses and to no other flowers. No one has a right to say, "To me this is not a rose". Heat, despite the different degrees of comfort or discomfort occasioned by it, can be measured by instruments. The words that stand as tokens for a rose or for heat illuminate the same patches in everyone's mind and illuminate them in the same way.

But some words are neither so amenable nor so definable. The vague but characteristic effulgence they shed over vast tracts of the mind marks them out as doing a very important duty, but doing it ineffectively. The word 'god', for example, can't be treated like half a crown. Its value has been debated since civilisation began, between men who consider it to be the major part of a man's banking account, men who regard it as worthless, and men who simply don't know what it is worth. And yet without the word the very debate would have been impossible.

Such words have always goaded sensitive men; it is irritating to find oneself in the presence of something that is both important and indefinable. Vast quantities of literature have come into being under the spur of this irritation: vast tracts of human experience have been examined. The word 'god' has focused man's mind on religion and the word 'beauty' on æsthetics. In each case the attempt has been to give the word an agreed value. And in each case the attempt has failed.

It was bound to fail. Confronted by the Sistine Madonna or the Blue Danube waltz, each man experiences different degrees of 'pleasure': confronted by a temperature of 80 degrees in the shade, each man suffers different degrees of physical comfort or discomfort. But no lover of painting or music can be confounded by a thermometer. He is himself the thermometer, and even though that does not affect the nature of the object that gave him the æsthetic sensation, he cannot determine its absolute æsthetic value. He can only point to the origin of his æsthetic pleasure, describe the pleasure he feels rather vaguely but with a degree of enthusiasm that leaves his sincerity in no doubt, and then conclude that the cause of his pleasure must be a thing of beauty—that which, being seen, pleases.

The syllogism contains a fatal flaw which any student of logic would note with glee. "A seen-thing-that-pleases is beautiful. This thing that I see pleases me. Therefore it is beautiful." How much more satisfactory it would be to say, "Beauty consists in X-ness. There is an unusual percentage of X-ness in this thing. Therefore this thing is unusually beautiful." The omission of the first person singular from the second argument makes it logically flawless. It also makes it useless, because of the lack of any instrument for measuring X-ness. The first argument falls back on the first person singular, and again the argument is invalidated, since it makes the quality it attempts to define depend on the perceiver and not on the thing perceived. "Therefore it is beautiful *to me*" is the only possible conclusion. "To you it is a rose: to me it is my heart," says the song writer, thus making it clear once for all that the value of the 'it' in question depends on whether a botanist or a lover is speaking.

But logic, that rather clumsy machine for detecting fallacies, can never succeed in discovering truth. Having exposed St. Thomas's fallacy, and having raised a pair of shocked eyebrows on finding that so good an Aristotelian should have paid so little attention to his master's teaching, logic may retire. Logic can get rid of a certain amount of encumbering dead wood, but whoever attempts to analyse beauty is concerned with a living growth. And for that another method must be used.

It is clear then that an enquiry into the nature of visual beauty must be prepared to examine two sets of phenomena—the quality itself and the emotion it produces. It is equally clear that the presence of the quality is only revealed by the presence of the emotion. And one might easily be tempted to conclude that, since the only proof that beauty exists at all is the fact that human beings are susceptible to its power, therefore the only clue to its nature is to be found in an analysis of the emotions. That is surely the pit into which most of the writers on æsthetics have disappeared: the fruits of their labours have been rather psychological than æsthetic. To write a book on the æsthetic emotions in the hope that it will shed light on the nature of beauty seems to me rather like examining the construction of a mirror in the belief that by so doing the nature of the universe reflected in it will be revealed.

Certainly if our only proof that the universe existed were that we possessed a mirror that reflected it (and there is a school of thought which would consider that to be a fair, though possibly an over-simplified, statement of the truth), science would be under an obligation to make a scrupulous examination of the mirror before coming to any conclusions about the reality of the phenomena reflected therein. Equally, the æsthetician is bound to consider very carefully what processes take place in the beholder who is brought in contact with a thing of beauty. But that is merely a preliminary step, and one that many philosophers and psychologists have taken. To stop there is to take note of the symptoms of a disease without enquiring into its cause.

Plenty of research has been done on the nature of the symptoms. It is not my intention to add to it, but it will be useful to enumerate some of its more obvious features. Pleasure, as St. Thomas pointed out, is its recognisable characteristic. Beauty is a desirable commodity. But not all men are equally susceptible to it. Nor are all men agreed about its abode. Moreover, it varies with period. It is subject to the laws that govern fashion. The unadorned horizontal rhythms of a modern block of flats produce unmistakable symptoms in the twentieth century. No such symptoms would be observable if the generations that produced Rheims Cathedral were confronted with the same block of flats. Sir Christopher Wren's contemporaries would have been even more impervious.

It also varies with its geographical position. What is beautiful in England is not necessarily so in India, still less in New Guinea. Variations in national or racial standards of beauty are as noticeable as in period standards.

All this is common knowledge. It would hardly be worth noting were it not that, however obvious, it tends to be forgotten as soon as the enquiring mind begins to concentrate on the particular case. Variations in personal sensitivity can easily be accounted for. Sensitivity is largely begotten by experience, yet human beings continue to quarrel among themselves as to what is or is not beautiful, rather than to ask who is or is not capable of recognising beauty. Variations in period-sensitivity can be analysed with some degree of accuracy, and a set of conclusions can be drawn from them in which the type of beauty acceptable to a given period is seen to be the result of an inevitable chain of causes and effects, which ensures that the Zeitgeist shall always find its expression in the taste of the period. And yet the appearance of a new link in the chain, bringing with it a new set of rhythms or curves or colour harmonies, invariably causes confusion —not merely an inability to recognise the new form of expression as beautiful (that would be understandable), but an emphatic denial that it is beautiful; an assertion that because the rash has not appeared the bacillus does not exist. If therefore we regard beauty as a quality whose presence is only revealed whenever it is reflected in the mirror of the human soul, we must admit at the outset that the mirrors that reveal it are extremely imperfect: that the majority of them are not sufficiently polished nor sufficiently coated with mercury to give a satisfactory reflection: that even if only those that are well polished and well coated are taken into account, we still find remarkable variations dependent both on time and place: and that in the case of the present day we are dealing with a set of mirrors that are only half constructed.

Having made these admissions, it becomes clear that the scientist's approach—the method of collecting the maximum amount of evidence and then constructing a theory that will account for it—is of little use. The evidence of defective mirrors and half-made mirrors is useless. The scientific method, applied to the rough-and-tumble of everyday life, has been called 'Mass Observation'—a method I both mistrust and dislike because it is too closely concerned with 'the average', 'the typical', 'the normal'. If beauty can only be measured in terms of sensitivity, then let us by all means ignore all but the most sensitive men when we are collecting our data.

Nevertheless, the Mass Observation method has its uses. Like a map, it enables one to take in wide stretches of country and note their main features. For detail it is useless, but it can provide a useful framework for detail. I confess that I have done very little by way of research into the 'average' man's reaction to beauty, nor have I drawn up tabulated lists of the objects or experiences that the 'average' man considers exceptionally beautiful. I am fairly sure that to do so would add very little to the data that one normally accumulates in the course of one's experience. A set questionnaire often defeats its own object by inducing a self-conscious habit of mind in the questionee, especially if he is called upon to analyse his sensations rather than his actions. "How many potatoes do you usually eat every day?" can be safely asked without setting up a too violent defensive reaction; but "How much trouble would you take to see a Picasso Exhibition?" would probably twist the victim into an analytical state of mind that would distort the real facts. On the other hand, it is not difficult to find out what things give the average man and woman the most æsthetic pleasure; to what lengths the average man and woman will go in the pursuit of æsthetic pleasure; to what lengths he or she will go in order to avoid displeasure. One knows, for example, that certain kinds of music cause certain sorts of people to switch off their wireless sets; and finally, one knows that certain kinds of objects and experience strike different classes of people as being beautiful, and that in general what is known as 'good taste' seems to have some connection with what is known as 'education'.

These interesting variations do not in themselves prove that beauty exists purely in the eye of the beholder. A million different readings from a million defective or sluggish thermometers do not prove that heat exists only in the instrument subjected to it. What makes the question of 'good taste' loom so large in considering standards of beauty is the habit of regarding works of art as the only touchstones. For a reason that must later be analysed, 'taste' in certain kinds of experience is so little subject to variation that the word becomes almost unnecessary.

If pleasure is to be the only guide to beauty, and if one is looking for something that gives universal pleasure in order to point to something that can be universally acknowledged as beautiful, the search soon comes to an end. True, there are plenty of things that give universal (or almost universal) displeasure. Bad health, cold weather, vermin, insufficient food, the smell of drains—the list is long and sounds absurd, and the mere absence of these unpleasantnesses does not in itself produce positive pleasure. Normal well-being can be left out of account in this preliminary reconnaissance. But on the credit side the list is shorter, and many of its items are open to debate. Certain natural phenomena are fairly universally recognised as more pleasurable than others—well-wooded country as opposed to moor-land, mountains as opposed to plains, bright colours as opposed to dull ones—again the list could be extended indefinitely. But here the debate begins. Not everyone prefers Switzerland to Holland or a carpet of bluebells to a hayfield. The word 'taste' rears its enigmatic head again, and the question 'What *is* beauty?' begins to nag.

It begins to nag, but quite mildly. Devotees of the Fen Country do not usually lose their tempers with admirers of the Cotswolds. Nor do such devotees noticeably correspond to social or intellectual strata of society. 'Taste' in scenery is apparently not developed by education, nor have I often heard it suggested that there is such a thing as 'good taste' in scenery. Preferences are certainly developed by habit. The habit of close observation of a certain type of scenery develops into love, and love implies preference. But no one would suggest that the love of Lincolnshire was in itself more reasonable than the love of Gloucestershire, or that a more sensitive perception was demanded by the Black Forest than by the Bay of Naples.

The distinction between 'taste', which implies a preference for one set of characteristics as against another equally valid set, and 'good taste', which is a preference for characteristics which are presumed to be somehow more admirable in themselves than others, is an immensely important one. Preferences must be based on love, and love itself must be based on a set of values recognised, consciously or unconsciously, by the lover. Here or hereabouts are the roots of the problem of beauty. If those values, those initial stirrings of human perception and understanding which engender love, prove themselves in the end to be out of the range of analysis, then this book will have failed to move an inch nearer to the meaning of beauty or to explain the strange delight that a waterfall, a scent, a progression from tonic to dominant, a pattern of scarlet and gold, can give. I believe that analysis is possible; and I believe that such analysis must begin by recognising a difference in kind between 'taste' and 'good taste'. If that difference exists, it must correspond to a difference between two sorts of beauty which themselves differ in kind. If that essential distinction can be established, the possibility of discovering the true nature of beauty will have been brought perceptibly nearer.

The word 'love', which made its inevitable appearance in the last two paragraphs, was bound to arrive sooner or later. As soon as the individual becomes himself the measure of whatever subject may be under discussion, it turns out in the end that his only method of testing the results of his measuring is his capacity for love. Leave the individual out of the argument: substitute for him a machine made of glass tubes and mercury and a graduated scale, and you can dispense with the word. Otherwise no.

The word is not merely pregnant. It has a massiveness that includes a hundred meanings, graded from mild preference to insistent demand, and a hundred effects on human conduct between unobtrusive kindliness and wild self-sacrifice. It is a great bundle of threads that entwine themselves with every phase of human conduct. Question the meaning of any scrap of human activity from the digging of a garden or the drawing-up of a title deed to the painting of a picture, the founding of an empire or the sacking of a city, and one of the threads emerges.

Why does the gardener dig?

Because the soil must be prepared for the herbaceous border.

But why want an herbaceous border?

18

Because at the appointed season it will produce delphiniums and antirrhinums.

But why does he want delphiniums and antirrhinums?

Because—well, because they are beautiful.

More beautiful than the untilled soil?

Of course.

What makes them so? By what *law* is the blue of a delphinium more beautiful than the brown of the earth? By what *law* is the shape of an antirrhinum more beautiful than that of a clod of soil?

I don't know. It's preferable somehow.

Preferable? The man digging prefers blue to brown, antirrhinum shape to clod shape. Why?

Well, he just does. He *likes* delphiniums and antirrhinums.

He *likes*! Look at him: muddy boots, sweat on his forehead, dirty clothes, tired muscles. All that just for a liking of what he hopes will happen six months hence? Surely liking is a feeble word? Surely he loves the flowers? But what makes a man love these things as yet unborn, so that he is now making a navvy of himself for their sake? Is there a reason for this love? Is it possible to draw up a list of lovabilities with reasons *why* they are desirable?

Here the reader may justifiably point out that I am confusing the enthusiasm of the lover with that of the creator. That the real reason why the gardener takes so much trouble is not that he wants to *enjoy* his garden, but that he wants to *make* it: that he is an artist and not a connoisseur—a producer, not a consumer, of beauty. I agree. But that does not invalidate my argument. The gardener creates in order that he may enjoy. The fact that he is a creative artist merely means that he is so convinced that delphiniums are preferable to soil that he is prepared to acquire skill and to sacrifice time and comfort in order to ensure that he gets them. And if, in such a case, the word 'preference' carries with it such an urgency of meaning, then the word 'love' can justifiably be substituted for it.

Have I slipped into the trap that so easily caught the philosophers? Am I still playing this game of chess with my Creator, using words for pawns and triumphantly crying 'check' when I substitute my 'lovability' for his 'beauty'? I think not. Surely I have made one small step forward. Surely the mechanism of love, that delicate relationship between the lover and the object of his affections, provides a kind of key to this locked door at which so many philosophers have hammered. For the lover never doubts that the object of his affections—be it a delphinium or a girl or a god—*deserves* his love. His attention is centred, not on his own besotted state of mind, but on the qualities in the beloved that produced it. And to the blind non-lovers who complain that he is wasting good affections on an unworthy object, he will reply with a detailed and spirited analysis of the qualities that have enthralled him. We are accustomed to laugh at his analysis. What he takes for his beloved's powers of repartee, we know to be merely a social manner; what seems to him intelligence is, to us, second-hand cliché: what appears to him natural charm, we recognise as the well-known snare of the siren. Certainly he may be a myopic imbecile. But he has at least had the courage to attempt that description of X-ness which the æstheticians have usually shirked. Even though he may be the victim of an elaborate set of illusions, he has drawn up his list of lovabilities instead of explaining that he is in a condition of 'empathy'. He has transferred his attention from his own state of mind to the object that produced it.

There is, of course, a difference between the gardener-delphinium type of love and the Romeo-Juliet relationship: the former is an emotional current that flows in one direction only, while the latter mysteriously operates in two directions. Unlike Juliet, the delphinium has no emotional attitude to her lover or to other potential lovers, with the delightful result, often pointed out by æstheticians, that her beauty kindles no possessive instinct in man. There is no need to fight for a place in the delphinium's heart: there is no fear that she will give herself to another and a more ardent gardener. The only struggle— and it is one that never seems to ruffle the complacency of the æstheticians—is to develop and preserve the maximum sensitivity to the loveliness of the flower, the struggle to keep the æsthetic appetite keen.

If, then, one is to discover by the method of Mass Observation what things are to be called beautiful, and why, one must listen carefully to the recitals of lovers as they describe the perfections that have inflamed them. And if one is to understand their recitals one must be, quite frankly, a lover oneself. There is no difficulty there. The world is full of delphiniums and gods, all waiting for their human victims. But it is less easy for the victim to stand outside himself and analyse with a reasonable amount of detachment the emotion he feels—to account for it, to justify it, above all to prove that what he has assumed to be genuine charm is *not* the snare of the siren. To do so successfully, to submit the beloved object to the cold scrutiny of analysis and still to regard it as primarily lovable—to catalogue and describe it without losing sight of its lovability is difficult. In order to do so one must both feel and *think* about it. One must be both attached and detached, though it is not necessary to be both at the same time. Detachment must succeed attachment, but at exactly the right interval. In fact, here the analyst is faced with the same problem as the artist, of keeping his enthusiasm at full pressure and yet not allowing himself to be carried away by it. He must take his stand at the central point between the extreme of Romanticism and the extreme of Classicism. The Romantic observer pins his faith on feeling and cares little whether its impact disturbs the nice balance of his analysis: the Classic preserves his detachment and runs the risk of losing some of the original intensity of his emotion. Wordsworth's plea for "emotion recollected in tranquillity" is not the creed of a Classicist insisting on an emotional head of steam to drive the poetic engine. It is the voice of the Romantic studiously reminding himself that the molten metal of fine frenzy, the raw material of his art, will not set in the poetic mould until it has cooled a little.

If beauty is to be classified into genera and species, pinned down and labelled like a butterfly, it is particularly important that the metal should be taken just at the right moment of cooling. Taken too soon, the result is sentimental gush, formless enthusiasm. Taken too late, the result is an æsthetic system in which beauty is a mere intractable lump, as cold as the moon and as distant as the stars.

So much for the spirit in which the enquiry must be undertaken. Now for the nature of the enquiry into beauty itself. Let me return to that ultimate starting-point where St. Thomas Aquinas sits doggedly at his desk asserting that beauty is that which, being seen, pleases. What are the consequences of his bald statement?

Beauty, says St. Thomas, gives pleasure to the beholder. If you want to track beauty to her lair, find a man who is pleased, discover what has pleased him, and you have a sample of beauty.

Yes, but what *process* has caused his pleasure? What has happened inside him to turn an image on his retina into a feeling of happiness in his brain (or his mind, or his soul, or what you will)? It is certainly not his eye that is pleased. Surely one thing only can cause pleasure or increase it—namely, the gratification of a desire. He *wanted* something, this man who has just seen and been pleased with what he saw. He had a hunger, and his hunger has been satisfied.

If pleasure is the result of gratified desire, then, if one could only look into a man's mind, find out just what desires are lurking there, and note the exact shape of the vacuum that needs filling; whatever would exactly fit the hollow spaces would, for him at least, be made in the shape of beauty's own self.

Desires are not accidents. They are conditioned by habit. The man with no experience of light has no hunger for light: therefore he can have no pleasure in light. The man who has never seen a tree, smelled the earth after rain, heard the thrush sing or the waves break, felt the sun on his cheek, can never long for such things. His desires are the outcome of his experience.

St. Thomas's man is only pleased by the sight of things that are like, or rather like, the things he has already experienced. His notion of what is beautiful is conditioned by his memory of what he has already seen, heard, smelled, felt, tasted. This, surely, turns the argument upside-down. We can no longer conclude that a thing is beautiful because A likes it. We must say that A's experience of life has given him certain appetites, and that things *become* beautiful in proportion to their power to satisfy his ever-changing appetites. For he is always accumulating new experiences. Every day brings him a new sight or sound, and every new sight or sound gives him a new hunger.

"But," the reader may object, "can a man only like things with which he is already familiar? Are there no basic hungers? Doesn't the baby thrill with æsthetic pleasure at the first contact of its lips with its mother's breast? And can the grown man take no pleasure in the sight of his first mountain or his first sunset?" Unfortunately the baby can give no evidence beyond a gurgle which his parents choose to interpret as an expression of inner bliss. Moreover, even in the womb, the baby has already known hunger and acquired the habit of appeasing it. But the evidence of adults shows conclusively that experience and desire are intimately connected. Love (of which desire, the will to take, is one half) is engendered almost entirely by habit. Patriotism, for example, is almost universal, and patriotism is hardly more than the result of a life spent in a certain environment. The Italian acquires a love of olive trees and blue sky through the constant sight of them, of spaghetti by the constant taste of it. These and a hundred similar loves combine to produce a love of Italy which pure reason cannot defend. For pure reason can never prove that an olive is in itself more lovable than an oak. The woman whom the native of Uganda regards as beautiful is based on the women he has seen in Uganda, just as the English man's type of female beauty is based on English women. There can be no fixed standard of beauty where there is no common fund of experience.

Granted, then, that beauty is conditioned by appetite and appetite by familiarity, much still remains to be discovered. Things are certainly not equally beautiful because they are equally familiar. Pigs and horses are equally common objects of the countryside, thistles are commoner than wild roses, blades of grass are commoner than thistles. How is one to account for the conviction that such things possess different *degrees* of visual beauty? It is useless to suggest that some things are better proportioned than others, more harmoniously shaped, better in colour. Whence do we derive our standards of proportion, shape or colour? Unless we can refer to some such standard, who has the right to assert that a pig's legs are too short? Too short for what? For the pig? Obviously not that, or pigs would have developed longer legs in the course of evolution. For beauty? But the legs on a chest of drawers are even shorter, and yet no one objects that a chest of drawers is inherently ugly. It is easy to say that a horse's neck is nobly curved, but what constitutes nobility of curvature? Can one kind of curve be noble in its own right and another lacking in nobility? And what if one were to discover, on looking more closely, that the curve of a horse's neck was identical with the curve of a pig's backside?

Questions of this kind may seem tiresomely academic. I have a good deal of sympathy with the man who is content to prefer a horse to a hippopotamus without wanting to know why. Even if the reason why could be demonstrated mathematically, what difference would it make to him? The horse would be no nobler, the hippopotamus no less uncouth. At first sight it would seem a waste of time and thought to puzzle out laboriously and rationally what the eye can grasp instinctively and effortlessly. But when one remembers that this remarkable capacity of the eye to appraise the beauty of Nature breaks down when confronted with works of art, and breaks down so completely that no æsthetic yardstick can be discovered that will satisfy even two experts, the question becomes less academic. The difference between a horse and a hippopotamus is in some way not the same as the difference between a Titian and a Picasso. Yet the two differences must be examined and contrasted before we can realise what kind of problem confronts us. And if neither Picasso nor Titian can put brush to canvas until they have stocked their visual memories with the shapes of horses and hippopotami, and the colours of earth and delphiniums, it follows that this preliminary question of man's experience of Nature, however academic it may seem, must be tackled before approaching the more difficult problem of man's attitude to art.

So much for our preliminary stalking of the word. The reconnaissance has done nothing by way of storming the citadel, but it has suggested a plan by which the citadel may be stormed—to think of the beautiful as a special variety of the lovable, in which the emotional traffic moves in one direction only; and to realise that the lover must not only be (as he always is) articulate but also in full possession of his analytical faculties.

Roughly speaking, it would seem then that such standards of beauty as exist are formed by a man's personal experience of the visible world. Visual experience builds up a vast stock of visual memories, and the visual memories bring in their train a set of corresponding visual appetites. The visual experiences are, as it were, a set of solid objects: the visual memories are like moulds of those objects—hollows waiting to be filled. Only further experience can fill them. And only visual experiences of a similar shape will fill them satisfactorily. Experiences of a different shape will certainly occur, but until they have in their turn produced visual memories and visual appetites, they will not be recognised as pleasurable. What, then, has to be done in any analysis

of the nature of beauty is to examine the general nature of the phenomena that surround us and have formed our appetites; and, having
done so, to discover whether these phenomena are not governed by
determining laws. For it is the law behind the phenomenon that is all-
important. The human mind, surrounded by an extraordinary diversity
of experiences, soon begins to correlate them, to classify and reconcile
them and to discover their common factors. Instinctively it begins to
deduce a set of laws, and the riper the experience the more complex
the law deduced. Any experience which appears to contradict the law
is a disturbing, if not an intolerable, miracle. The sun rises every day—
a surprising phenomenon until one says to oneself "as regular as
clockwork", thereby postulating a clock or some equally rhythmic
mechanism to account for it. The phenomenon then ceases to surprise.
Then comes an eclipse of the sun: surprising again, until one postulates another clock with another rhythm and a longer pendulum.
Again surprise diminishes. The intolerable miracle has become another example of the law-abiding behaviour of the universe. The new
experience has made it necessary to discover another law to contain
the old law.

Beauty, I submit, can be described as law-abiding behaviour, and
the response to beauty an instinctive recognition of the existence of
law behind behaviour. There is no need to formulate the laws: all that
is necessary is a conviction that law exists, and that since it exists it
must manifest itself in some kind of pattern, and that in the ultimate
analysis every pattern can be expressed in terms of mathematics. The
origin of beauty is only to be found in a study of God's Geometry.
Finally, that Geometry must be examined at once passionately and
dispassionately. The thermometer must itself diagnose the cause of
the temperature. It is a task worth attempting.

To point to that mathematical basis is one half of the task—the
half that concerns itself with beauty in Nature. The other half concerns
itself with beauty in art. The pattern of the universe is of such extraordinary complexity that the human mind can never grasp it fully.
None the less, if the human mind does not grasp a portion of it, the
universe becomes meaningless. Or rather it becomes chaotic, and chaos
is the opposite of beauty. From time to time different aspects of the
pattern imprint themselves on the minds of exceptionally sensitive

men, and those men, in their endeavour to express their delight in what they have discovered, become great artists. These attempts of theirs are infectious; whole generations catch their enthusiasm, become more and more acutely conscious of the particular aspect the artist has revealed. Such mass enthusiasms have the effect of turning a floodlight on to some particular fragment of life, isolating it, simplifying it, intensifying it—making it lovable, and therefore beautiful. Once a small corner of it has been thoroughly illumined, posterity will always have a clearer vision of that corner even after the illumination has died down. But the universe is inexhaustible. The floodlights of the past, remarkable though they have been, have only picked out a negligible handful of the interwoven patterns that await discovery. It might have been thought that the Greek sculptors had turned such a fierce light on to the pattern-possibilities of the human body that nothing remained to be discovered. Yet the Italian Renaissance, approaching the same area of experience from another direction, discovered a set of pattern-possibilities undiscovered by the Greeks. Pheidias did not exhaust the mine. Michelangelo tapped another seam, Rubens another, Degas another. The whole world awaits the discovering eye of the artist. And once he has made his own fragment of discovery, he has thereby added to our sense of beauty. The phrase we use to explain this fundamental truth, "his work is beautiful", is a misleading phrase. It presupposes that he has *created* beauty where none existed. What he has, in fact, done is to lift a corner of the veil and *reveal* beauty. The artist can no more create beauty than the scientist can create truth. The scientist measures relationships in the existing universe. The artist divines such relationships and restates them in clarified form. Both of them are engaged in 'understanding' the universe—the one using intellect, the other emotion. Both of them make extracts from the universe. The scientist's extract is called 'truth' and the artist's 'beauty'.

But it is clear that the complex 'pattern' of the universe, from which the artist's comparatively simple extract is made, has been arrived at by a process which has nothing to do with beauty. The only guiding principle in formulating that pattern is function. The pattern of the stars and of a nettle leaf are equally the result of the law of the survival of the fittest. The effort of the Galactic system to function as a Galactic

26

system, and of the nettle leaf to be an efficient nettle leaf, is the factor that decides their form, colour, movement and growth. The complexity of the resultant pattern arises from the interaction of different functions. For example, if the effort of a caterpillar to function as a caterpillar causes it to eat the nettle leaf, the pattern of the leaf will be spoiled. If anything interferes with the caterpillar's effort, the pattern of the caterpillar will be spoiled. To the human observer it is beauty that has been interfered with; to the designer of the universe it is merely that one function has been sacrificed to another.

Therefore the study of beauty in Nature involves the study of function—or at least a realisation that natural beauty is a by-product of function. Whereas the study of beauty in art involves no such thing. What causes the artist to extract a fragment of the universal pattern is his *love* of the pattern. He presents it to us purged of its functional trappings, as a thing admirable not because it *works* but because it *is*. The spiral of a nautilus shell is the inevitable result of the growth of the nautilus. From the laws of growth it derives its own mathematical formula. But the same spiral in a work of art is there merely because the curve pleased the artist's eye. He may have guessed intuitively at its mathematical basis, but his only excuse for using it is his delight.

Such is the argument this book intends to pursue. It can be summed up in a sentence. Beauty in Nature is a product of the mathematical behaviour of Nature, which in its turn is a product of function; whereas beauty in art is a product of man's love of, based on his intuitive understanding of, the mathematics of Nature.

That may sound a dull theme for a book until one remembers the extraordinary complexity of mathematics and the even more extraordinary intensity of love.

CHAPTER II

Nature

PHENOMENA—SOUNDS, SIGHTS, SMELLS, TASTES—CAN BE DIVIDED into two classes, natural and artificial. It is an important division. The difference, from the point of view of the beholder (or listener, smeller, toucher, taster), lies in a difference of intention. The intention behind natural phenomena cannot easily be criticised or questioned, since you, dear reader, and I are part of it. The clay might conceivably rebel against the potter's notion of a vase, for the potter did not make the clay. But since the Creator fashions both clay and potter, neither has the right to criticise the other. Only in exceptional moments of power-drunk egotism does man wish Nature otherwise. Here, for example, is the Duke of Dorset, gazing up at the steadfast thunder-clouds—"How nobly they had been massed for him! One of them, a particularly large and dark one, might with advantage, he thought, have been placed a little further to the left. He made a gesture to that effect. Instantly the cloud rolled into position. The gods were painfully anxious, now, to humour him in trifles." How carefully Max prepares one for the fantastic notion that perhaps once in a lifetime, and then only as a great treat, could the potter bow to the clay's puny sense of fitness, or the clay dare to criticise the hand that made it.

The cloud and the tree have been called into being by a set of forces quite unlike those which created the cathedral and the table. The forces that created the tree are also responsible for the creature who looks at it. The force that created the table is not.

The nature of man's intention when he designs and fashions a table is a very complex and surprising one. So also is the effect of the table on his fellow-men when they look at it or use it. They have the right to wish it otherwise, since they stand outside the intention that

28

produced it. And once they exercise that right, they begin to have what they are pleased to call 'good taste'. They are not part of the law that made the table. They have their own laws, and the tables *they* would fashion would be different tables. The bulk of this book will concern itself with those two strange phenomena—the creation of works of art by the artist and the enjoyment of them by his fellows. But this chapter must concern itself only with man's attitude to Nature. That must come first, for the basic fact is that man cannot make a table without first having experienced a tree. The tree is as much bound up with himself and the pattern of which he is a part as are two planets in the Solar System. If Neptune could modify or even protest against the weight and speed of Saturn, the delicate balance of the whole Solar System would be upset. Neptune itself would be involved in the consequent readjustment, for Neptune is only Neptune because Saturn is Saturn, and man is only man because a tree is a tree. Goodness knows what violent rearrangements had to be improvised throughout the whole created universe when that single thunder-cloud was moved to the left to please the ducal whim.

But if natural phenomena can neither be criticised (since there is no standard of values wherewith to compare them) nor altered with impunity (since they are so interdependent that a single alteration would upset their delicately adjusted balance), they can at least be examined dispassionately. Nature can be measured and described as a collection of phenomena. And it can be submitted to all manner of tests as a machine for producing phenomena.

That is the province of the scientist. He can measure the acorn and the oak tree, and he can describe the processes whereby the acorn becomes the oak tree. By doing so he can produce a good deal of useful material which the æsthetician can eventually use: the scientist's search for facts must precede the æsthetician's search for values. He has never ceased in that search since man began to be conscious that life could be examined and contemplated as well as lived and enjoyed.

It is sometimes disconcerting to the layman to note how meagre are the scientist's statistics and how little he has been able to understand the world he inhabits. But he has discovered a good deal, even though he has failed to solve the major mysteries. On the whole, he has been able to understand and describe the machinery of the universe, though not the power that keeps it in motion. He can describe the atomic texture of matter; he can watch the growth of organic tissue that turns a child into a man, an acorn into an oak, and the changes that occur in inorganic tissue whereby a handful of dust becomes a diamond. But he cannot understand the nature of life or death. He can neither describe them nor can he account for them. That is annoying. It would simplify the art critic's problem if he could go to the scientist for his data. "I am engaged on a study of the laws of beauty. I have decided that they are somehow dependent on the laws of Nature. Will you kindly give me a complete list of the laws of Nature with a brief description of how they work. I will then deduce from them the laws of beauty." The list, alas, can never be complete nor the description adequate. Nevertheless, the critic must do what he can with the incomplete list and the inadequate description. If science can only light half of his path, he can at least explore the illuminated portion. To do even that is something. Even a cul-de-sac is worth exploring.

As far as I know, the only writer who has seriously attempted the exploration is John Ruskin. He at least tried to examine phenomena in the light of his love of phenomena. But because his prose is weighty and involved, and because he is alleged to have confused beauty with truth and goodness, and because, like all lovers, he is articulate without being logical—and, above all, because he will allow no one to disagree with him but himself, he is little read to-day, though he has been emerging during the last few years from the shadow of prejudice that obscured him. And yet the five volumes of *Modern Painters* contain a great deal that is worth saying about beauty in Nature. For Ruskin did, very patiently, examine the laws that govern the visible world he undoubtedly loved. It was a limited world, romantically conditioned by the taste of the nineteenth century. Sunsets and torrents and towering alps alternate in it with crystals and flowers in the crannied wall. But it was, none the less, a world he had experienced intensely, and which had roused him to a pitch of enthusiastic curiosity that few writers have ever equalled. Ruskin felt that, since experience of the universe is the artist's raw material, some attempt to examine the universe must precede any enquiry into the nature of the arts.

That seems to me the only reasonable method of arriving at a solution of the two main problems—the problem of how it is that man's experience of Nature conditions his sense of what is and what is not beautiful: and the problem of why, within the limits of his experience, natural objects appear to possess greater or lesser degrees of beauty.

An acorn falls to earth and an inevitable chain of events is started. Laws so complex that they cannot be explained, so numerous that they cannot be counted, and so rigid that they cannot be broken, come immediately into operation. The combined result of these irresistible forces will eventually be an oak tree, a particular oak tree different from all other oak trees. It will owe its difference not to blind chance but to an unbroken sequence of causes and effects. Indeed, a scientist who had the knowledge and patience to estimate the quality of the soil, the direction of the prevailing wind, the rainfall, the variations of temperature, the hours of sunshine (each in its turn the result of another inescapable series of causes): who could deduce from these data the acorn's rate and direction of growth: who could guess at the probability of damage by lightning, earthquake or pests, or of interference by neighbouring oak trees protecting it from rain, depriving it of sun or sheltering it from wind: such a man might roughly predict the appearance of the oak tree at the end of an interval of, say, fifty years, at the very moment when the acorn struck its first rootlet into the ground. And what is true of the acorn is equally true of every cloud, every blade of grass, every mosquito and every mountain contour—not to mention every philosopher.

The result of obedience to law is uniformity. Isolate a single one of Nature's laws, cancel out the rest, and the result is a pattern. Conceive, for example, that the acorn has nothing to attend to beyond the law that compels it to struggle upwards, vertically, branching outwards at intervals at a given angle and at given intervals from the main stem. The result would be a world in which all oak trees were constructed on a geometrical pattern, a world of absolute symmetry and no surprises, the world of an engineer's drawing-board. But call into play one more law, the law of gravity, for example; let each branch feel a downward pull to counteract the upward struggle, and the uniformity, though still present, begins to be more interesting, the pattern more complex. At each point in the lateral branches the contest between growth and gravity produces a different result. According to their thickness and resilience, the branches begin to assume curves of the utmost subtlety. Call into play, one by one, each of the forces that our imaginary scientist has tried to estimate, and each will play its part in modifying the pattern of our original tree. The curve produced by growth-versus-gravity will again be modified by the impact of sunshine from the south, drawing the branch towards it, or by a wind from the west momentarily interfering with the pull of the earth. A raindrop clinging to the lower lobe of each leaf will modify each leaf's natural symmetry. Moss forming on the damp side of the trunk will upset the trunk's uniformity of colour. Till at last our oak tree, modelled on the simple ideal of the engineer's drawing-board, has submitted, in every square inch of its surface, to such countless variations from that ideal that the original simple design can only be dimly divined behind the variations. And yet each variation is no more than an additional act of obedience to still another law. It is not a negation of the drawing-board pattern; it is an interweaving with it of other related patterns.

Now, surely if the mind has a basic hunger, it is the hunger to understand and to correlate. The most irritating thing in the world, as Herodotus once pointed out, is to be full of thoughts and sensations, and yet not to be able to marshal and sort them out. That desire to come to grips with the incessant stream of impulses that pours along the sensory nerves from the sense organs to the brain *must* be gratified or life becomes intolerable. If my eye sends me nothing but reports of visual chaos, or apparent visual chaos, in the outer world, the part of my brain that receives visual messages will be in a permanent condition of distress. "There was never anything ugly or misshapen," said Sir Thomas Browne, "but the Chaos wherein, notwithstanding, to speak strictly, there was no deformity because no form." Submit that outer chaos to law, introduce that uniformity of behaviour which is the inevitable result of obedience to law, and at once the mental distress changes to pleasure. St. Thomas Aquinas's sensitive man finds himself pleased with what he has seen, and surely he is justified in assuming that the source of his pleasure—the thing he has been in the habit of calling beautiful, because he loved it and desired it, has an intimate connection with law, or at least with his recognition of the workings of law.

Such a recognition would account for a great deal. The human mind, finding itself surrounded by countless examples of law-abiding behaviour, begins to accept such behaviour as normal, then to expect it and be distressed at its absence—or apparent absence: for it never is absent—then to demand it, and finally to love it. It ties phenomena together into an intelligible whole; it imposes rhythm and pattern on the universe and relates the grain of sand to the mountain, the mosquito to the whale, and regulates the behaviour of molecules and spiral nebulæ alike.

The theme is a stimulating one for the scientific observer. No wonder that microscopes and telescopes, spectroscopes and thermometers, were busy during the nineteenth century examining, measuring, analysing and recording the behaviour of the universe. For the scientist nothing could be more exciting than to play the detective, examine the clues and discover the laws that made everything just so. And no wonder the religious enthusiast, endeavouring to carry the detective game into a sphere beyond the range of scientific instruments, found himself out of sympathy with the scientist because he had entered a sphere of enquiry in which measurement was impossible. Ruskinian attempts to reconcile the scientific and the religious approaches are rare and, in the opinion of the twentieth century, mainly unsuccessful. And yet if our objective is to be an examination of beauty, the two approaches must be reconciled. Neither the classic method of the scientist nor the romantic mood of the mystic will suffice. The first refuses to recognise beauty as a value, because it cannot be measured: the second refuses to recognise measurement as even desirable, and therefore cannot envisage beauty except as a cause of vague satisfaction.

But although it would be theoretically possible to explain the visible aspect of every natural phenomenon—its shape, size, colour and texture—in terms of a mathematical formula derived from a set of underlying laws, in practice the task of doing so would not only be infinitely laborious but utterly useless. Once it has been pointed out (and Plato pointed it out neatly enough in the *Philebus*) that beauty is ultimately reducible to mathematics and that the appreciation of beauty is ultimately dependent on one's recognition of the mathematical behaviour of the universe, all that is needed is to cite a few examples of complex rhythmic behaviour and note the infinite variety of resultant relationships between shape, size, colour and texture. Such relationships can only be grasped intuitively, and intuition is quite sufficient for their enjoyment. Even the scientist must approach his task intuitively, otherwise he will never be able to select the small portion of the universe which he wishes to measure, and, indeed, he will not be able to formulate a wish to measure one aspect rather than another. But the layman must rely on intuition alone, while the artist is only an artist because his intuitive understanding is so heightened as to merit the name of 'love'. And he has coined the word 'beauty' precisely because he wishes to stress the intuitive or amorous approach that can afford to dispense with measurement.

Nature provides very few instances of form whose mathematical basis the eye can grasp in its entirety and at a glance. One of the few is the logarithmic spiral of the nautilus shell whose mathematical formula is dependent upon the rate of growth of the nautilus, which constructs each new section of its abode to fit its new dimensions. Another is the perfect sphere of the soap bubble, which owes its shape to Nature's determination to enclose the maximum volume of air within the minimum area of containing surface. Certainly there is a mild satisfaction to be derived from the contemplation of perfect spheres and logarithmic spirals. Both are well within the range of the scientist's measuring instruments and the artist's intuition. But such simple geometry is mercifully rare. One has only to examine a square foot of vegetation in the nearest patch of hedgerow to find oneself in a world of colour and form-relationships that go far beyond the power of mathematics to explain. Even the mathematician who reduced the soap bubble to a simple mathematical formula, in which the surface tension of soap-solution and the "law of the minimum enclosing area" play their part, soon begins to find himself in deeper water as soon as two soap bubbles come together, and he has to examine the distortion to the spherical form that results when a common surface unites the two spheres. The formula is more elaborate, but is still well within his grasp, provided he ignores such complications as currents of air pressing sideways on the enclosing film. Three soap bubbles give him a still more complicated formula, and five almost baffle the human mind. And yet Nature rarely provides so simple a spectacle as a bunch of five soap bubbles.

The housewife who plunges her arms into a mass of ten thousand bubbles and, instead of guarding them reverently from any force that might disturb their surface tension, recklessly rinses her husband's shirt through the mass is setting up a series of shifting movements that are still governed by mathematics, but which would drive any mathematician who tried to find their formula into a premature grave. As for the foam that drifts across the back of every breaking wave—surely the most ardent mathematician would be overtaken by nausea

Hedgerow

at the very notion of referring its behaviour to mathematics. Yet only mathematics can explain it—it, and the tiger and the sunflower and the cumulus cloud and the tangle of grass in the hedgerow. That tangle is no more chaotic than the nautilus shell or the soap bubble, but it is more interesting because its pattern has been determined by the inter-action of many laws. Every flower and every grass stem in it is dis-posed to a fraction of a millimetre in a pattern that the eye delights to grasp, but which the mind can never hope to analyse. Each stem, as it thrusts upwards, is directed by the proximity of other stems and its own will to secure its share of light and air; its curve is the result of a balance between its length, its resilience (which varies in a mathematical progression throughout its length) and the weight of the seed that grows on the end of it. And each of these ingredients varies both in itself and in its relationship to the others, from day to day, as the sap rises, as the seed ripens. And since botanical classification divides the order Gramineæ into forty-six tribes, and each tribe contains an average of five species, there are between two and three hundred kinds of grass, each with its different stem-length, resilience and weight: each therefore producing a slightly different curve, each curve modified by its immediate environment.

If anyone doubts that an underlying orderliness is at work even in the most apparently chaotic patch of natural form, let him try the effect of interfering with such a patch. Let him, for example, tie up against a wall a stem of bramble that has been lying along the ground, or let him blast out a quarry from a hillside. Immediately his eye is afflicted with a sense of something amiss, of a pattern disturbed. The leaves that had arranged themselves so carefully to catch the sunlight are now disarranged and will require at least a week to reorganise themselves. The curvature of the hillside, the product of centuries, has lost its inevitability. At least a century will be required to repair these interferences with Nature's formulæ.

Under such circumstances it is evident that science and mathematics can do no more than offer a set of rough, though valuable, pointers. They can open a door to the jungle, but, once through the door, only intuition can find the way. The scientist can explain the sphere, the hexagon and the spiral; he can account for the soap bubble, the honeycomb and the nautilus shell. He can point out that Nature's tendency to produce spherical and circular forms, owing to the "law of minimum containing areas," also tends to result, owing to the "law of tight packing" and Nature's disinclination to waste space, in hexagonal planes and solids with an hexagonal section. For the next regular unit of circles is a unit of seven—a central circle with six surrounding circles, each touching its neighbours and the central circle (Fig. 1). And when, as in the case of the honeycomb, a number of these new units are being formed simultaneously, the pressure from each unit on its neighbour tends to flatten the sides into a hexagon, or a tightly packed colony of hexagons in which only the free outer surfaces are allowed to retain the circular section they long for (Fig. 2). He can thus account for Nature's supply of angles of 120°, just as he can account for angles of 90° by the law of gravity which, working at right angles to the horizontal surface of the earth, compels, for example, all growing things to achieve their equilibrium by progressing vertically. If, in a growing plant, the force of gravity is modified by the addition of centrifugal force, the direction of growth is distorted.

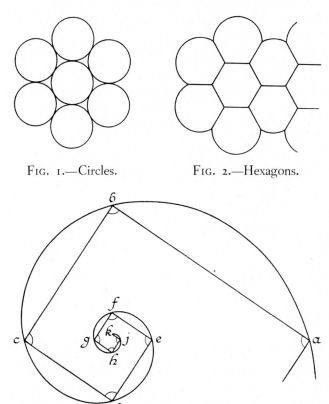

Fig. 1.—Circles.   Fig. 2.—Hexagons.

Fig. 3.—Logarithmic Spiral.

As for the logarithmic spiral produced by most shells and found throughout organic nature, as for example in the ram's horn, the mathematical formula, dependent on rate of growth, is one of the few that can be seen at work in largish objects. It arises from a geometrical progression (e.g. 1, 2, 4, 8, 16, 32, etc.). Draw a series of lines with lengths thus related to each other and joining each other at a constant angle; connect the angles with a curve, and the result is a logarithmic spiral.

The scientist can point out too that leaves, which share the general tendency to be circular, are thwarted in that desire by the intervention of other forces, which he can measure but cannot always understand. The nasturtium leaf is roughly circular. Like most leaves, it is composed of flattish surfaces stretched between a series of radiating ribs; but some force compels the ribs to grow more slowly in proportion as their angle diverges from that of the central rib which continues the line of the stem on which the leaf is supported. The result is still a rough circle, but a circle supported at a point which is not its exact centre.

With a lupin leaf another force comes into play—a force that for some reason contradicts the law of "minimum enclosing edges" and demands a larger contour in proportion to the area enclosed. This contradictory force produces a leaf of greater complexity than that of the nasturtium: and the more the force asserts itself the greater will that complexity be. The serrations of the buttercup or the delphinium leaf are more complex than those of the lupin. The thistle finds it necessary to weave backwards and forwards three-dimensionally, while the parsley and curly greens carry the same process to fantastic lengths.

But all this is mere kindergarten stuff. The soap bubble, the honeycomb and even the parsley are mathematically explicable. They offer elementary problems in natural geometry compared with the tiger, the oak tree or the breaking wave. Yet the difference is only one of degree. From the point of view of natural science, they too are expressible in terms of a mathematical formula. True, the formula would be too long and wearisome for the human mind to grasp, but the point I wish to establish is that the size, shape, colour and behaviour of a tiger conform just as rigidly to a set of inescapable laws as do those of the soap bubble; and that though the bubble can for practical purposes be reduced to statistics while the tiger cannot, they are both well within the grasp of human intuition. Indeed, intuition only begins to enjoy itself somewhere about the point where measurement is getting out of

38

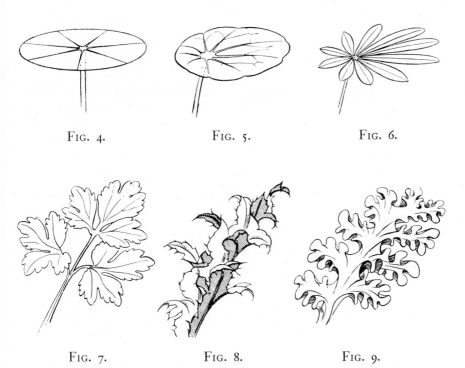

FIG. 4.   FIG. 5.   FIG. 6.

FIG. 7.   FIG. 8.   FIG. 9.

its depth. It can follow the regular sequence of rhythmic changes in the form and progress of the breaking wave: it can divine the *geo-metrically* diminishing intensity of colour between the foreground and the remote distance of a landscape owing to the density of the atmosphere. And in doing all this it can *know* that it is in contact with a mathematical world without needing to reduce its knowledge to statistics.

But intuition is concerned with something besides knowledge. It is concerned with enjoyment. And in proportion as it enjoys as well as knows, it adds *value* to *fact*. The moment the human being begins to examine preferences as well as things, he has moved into a realm in which the word 'beauty' has to be added to his vocabulary. But because he has examined things as well as preferences, the word 'beauty' will have for him a more stable foundation, a more explicit meaning. Knowing that beauty and mathematics are related, he will be able to save himself a good deal of time by trying to define what the relationship is and to avoid the error of assuming the truth of the very thing he wishes to prove—thereby arguing in a circle.

Even Ruskin allows himself to be drawn into this kind of error. In Section 1 of the second volume of *Modern Painters* (written in 1845), he made a serious attempt to analyse the nature of beauty; in 1883 he re-read what he had written and added a series of notes, of which the following is an extract from a note on his chapter on 'Typical Beauty': "I ought to have given one or two typical examples of the practical application of the foregoing section: and to have shown how, for instance, a wild rose is pretty because it has concentric petals—because each petal is bounded by varying curves—because the curves are dual and symmetrically opposed, and because the five petals are bent into the form of a cup," etc. All of which is meaningless until it has been proved that concentricity, variation of curvature, symmetry and so on are in themselves beautiful. The argument that a rose is pretty because it is like a cup merely prompts the question, "Why is a cup pretty?" Doubtless Ruskin did not think it worth while to labour what seemed to him obvious, but he was certainly under an obligation to show *why* concentricity is preferable to eccentricity and symmetry to asymmetry.

In attempting to discover such 'whys', one can only work backwards, noting and collecting types of form acknowledged as beautiful, and then analysing their mathematical origin. But to do so is certainly possible. If, for example, the Mass Observation method were to disclose (as I suspect it would) a general agreement that a nasturtium leaf is pleasanter to contemplate than a plain green circle set at right angles to a stem that joins it in the exact centre, and that a lupin leaf is pleasanter than a nasturtium, it would be safe to deduce that—other things being equal—the interaction of two laws produces beauty more easily than the operation of one, that the interaction of three laws is more potent still, and so on, up to that point when the pattern becomes too complex to grasp. And then, remembering the rather irritating fussiness of the parsley and the curly green, one could add a rider to the effect that the laws must be fairly evenly balanced. When one law gets the bit between its teeth at the expense of the others, the result is eccentric and therefore disturbing.

So far, then, one can say that beauty is the underlying mathematical behaviour of phenomena apprehended intuitively. And that it varies objectively with the number of interactive laws and the resultant mathematical complexity, and subjectively with the intuition of the beholder. In view of that clumsy but accurate statement, Ruskin's note on the wild rose will have to be worded rather differently. Is it true that a wild rose is pretty *because* it has concentric petals? If one accepts Ruskin's 'because' as the operative word, then an orchid or a sweet pea must be the reverse of pretty in so far as they are not concentric in plan. If a rose's cup-shaped section is the *cause* of beauty, then perhaps the lily's wine-glass-shaped section may rob it of beauty. But if one takes the circular plan and the cup-shaped section as a simple mathematical basis for a flower, one of many possible different but equally satisfactory bases, but needing a good deal more added complexity before it can be accepted as beautiful, then one is entitled to use the word 'because'. A rose, one can say, is beautiful because it contains (1) the perfect symmetry of a circle, partially contradicted by (2) the imperfect symmetry of a pentagon, reinforced by (3) the bilateral symmetry of each of its five petals, which makes tolerable (4) the subtlety of the curve that bounds each petal, plus (5) the cup-shaped section: the whole being given unity by its (6) pink colour, which in its turn is given a slight variety of tone by (7) a deepening of the colour towards the centre, and a slight variety of texture by (8) the contrast between the smooth surface of the petals and the rough core of stamens in the centre. In other words, there are eight different visual elements for the eye to grasp, and no single one of them has obtained the upper hand. Indeed, so evenly balanced are they that the element of surprise or slight discomfort is missing. Hence Ruskin uses the word 'pretty' rather than 'beautiful'. Had he chosen an orchid, the word would have been inappropriate.

This brings me to a second condition for beauty, one that will be of immense importance when we come to examine the meaning of the word 'taste'. A certain percentage of apparent disobedience must take place among the prevailing obedience: an admixture of unintelligibility among the intelligibility, of surprise among the familiar and the expected. The intuition in its perpetual assessment of æsthetic values must occasionally be baffled, or it will become bored and lose its sensitivity. Hence it is necessary that among the roses there should be an occasional orchid, whose pattern is a little more difficult to grasp. Or the elements of the familiar and baffling may even be mixed in a single object to provide the correct balance between the pretty which is not baffling enough and the bizarre which is too baffling. A simple, easily intelligible shape, like the laurel leaf, can be made more interesting by the addition of a slightly baffling pattern of spots. In the more difficult shape of the buttercup leaf, such a pattern would be too disturbing.

Fig. 10.   Fig. 11.

Doubtless it would be possible to discover exactly what the necessary percentage of unfamiliarity is, for it must be fairly constant both in art and Nature. With regard to Nature, which presents a spectacle more or less familiar to everyone, there is little divergence of opinion, and such divergence as exists will probably be largely the result of local conditions. To the Dutchman, accustomed to level plains, the unfamiliar element will take the form of an occasional mountain; to the inhabitant of a mountainous region an occasional expanse of level country would provide the necessary slight shock; but in art the case is different, for the extent and intensity of each man's experience of works of art varies enormously, and each man, according to the extent of his experience, will have a different norm of familiarity and therefore a different set of requirements to provide him with the necessary shock. The percentage of unfamiliarity he needs will be the same in each case, but the stylistic idioms with which he is familiar will be different. To the man who accepts the idiom of the Venetian High Renaissance as the norm, the distortions of el Greco will be sufficient to satisfy his needs, and those of Picasso will go far beyond them. He will therefore be stimulated by el Greco and disgusted by Picasso. This phenomenon must, however, be more fully discussed in a later chapter. Here I am concerned to note only that one of the necessities for beauty is a slight admixture of unfamiliarity or unintelligibility in the mass of familiarity or intelligibility. In the examination of single and smallish objects like leaves or flowers, this admixture is important. As soon as the eye tackles larger composite units, containing more visual elements—a wide stretch of country, for example—the balance of familiar with unfamiliar is almost sure to adjust itself automatically, since familiarity is the result of repetition and Nature will almost always provide enough apparent exceptions to her own rules in any given landscape.

A good test for beauty of form can be found in the conformation of mountains which have been shaped by the coming together of a vast number of natural forces. Stratified rock is horizontally deposited, then tilted and broken into masses by volcanic energy, then possibly smoothed and moulded by glacial action, and finally carved into subtler subsidiary shapes by streams whose action varies with the pace and volume of the water and the varying resistances or brittlenesses of the rock over which they flow, and which still further modify the original curvature by depositing and rearranging the debris they carve out of the main mass. The resultant forms are capable of infinite variety, beautiful or less beautiful in proportion to the balance of forces that have been at work. The foothills, for example, in the Isère valley near Grenoble have a slightly unsatisfactory character because the stratification is too insistent, and the subsequent tilting and breaking seems not to have been modified by the action of streams. There is too great a preponderance of straight lines, too little admixture of curvature. The mountains of the Savoy alps, on the other hand, that rise behind these foothills, are thoroughly satisfactory. But take in both foothills and alps at a single glance, as one easily can from half-way up the opposite side of the valley, and the slight uncouthness of the foothills gives an added piquancy, the piquancy of a musical discord, to the whole.

Or, to take a more extreme case, mountains like Etna or Fujiyama which have been formed by a single, simple process—namely, the steady flow of lava radiating from a central crater till the mountain has built itself up into an almost perfect cone—such mountains are in themselves tedious to the eye, since their form is too obvious to provide sufficient exercise for the analytical faculty. But since they occur so rarely as to constitute exceptions, they acquire beauty by the very fact of their unfamiliarity. A countryside dotted with them would be wearisome in the extreme.

It is this perpetual balance of competing elements in Nature which determines the shape of our æsthetic appetites and our consequent assessment of what is or is not beautiful in Nature. To analyse or even to catalogue typical examples would be useless. It is sufficient for my purpose to catalogue their kinds.

Form, in its own right, I have already glanced at, merely to show how inexhaustible are its possibilities. But in addition to isolated form there is that subdivision of form known as texture which can vary from the gloss of calm water through the matt surface of a meadow to the roughness of a pebbled shore.

Proportion—a convenient shorthand word to express relationships of size—plays an unsuspectedly important part in visual experience, being an inevitable product of function. For example, the thickness of an animal's legs relative to the bulk of its body is a function of the strength of bone. The elephant, reduced to the size of a horse, would at once appear inappropriately proportioned, for the eye has already divined the mathematical proportion underlying the construction of both animals. The proportions that are correct in a butterfly would be grotesque in a bird. Even the angles which seem natural in the chain of the Alps would be unconvincing in the Lake District.

Finally, the phenomenon of colour, which, partly because of its importance but mainly because in certain fundamental respects it is different in kind from the phenomenon of form, must be dealt with at greater length.

Colour as a product of function is a far more difficult problem to grasp even intuitively, and I suspect that what is called 'beauty' of colour in Nature may depend on a kind of mathematics that has never been properly understood and which I have no intention of analysing.

In one sense the phenomenon of colour lends itself to more strictly scientific examination than the phenomena of shape or mass, since it can more easily be isolated in the laboratory and submitted to experimental treatment. Hence the number of books from Newton's *Opticks* onwards setting forth theories of colour. Since, however, most of these are based on spectrum analysis and the examination of transmitted light—light coloured by the transparent objects through which it passes—they are of little use to the man who is concerned with normal visual experience, which is mainly the effect of remitted light—light coloured by opaque objects which throw it back.

"Normal visual experience," as far as colour is concerned, is extremely strange and complicated. For although colour and form are both 'properties' of any given object—a leaf is heart-shaped and it is also green—yet somehow one feels that form is a more inalienable property than colour, since colour is more subject to interference than is form. The greenness of a leaf may become blueness in the far distance, or purpleness in shadow, or even redness at sunset.

These interferences are of course easily explained when we remember that the apparent colour of an object is the result of a combination between its own 'local' colour and that of the light that falls on it; and that under circumstances where the colour of light can be controlled— in the theatre for example, where coloured gelatines can be interposed between the source of light and the illuminated object—an abnormal set of chromatic conditions can be artificially created with the greatest ease.

'Normal conditions', both for the scientist in the laboratory and the layman in the open air, consist of what is known as 'white light' falling on what are known as 'coloured' objects. For the scientist a vast field of research is open in both directions. Since Newton's *Opticks* was written, the behaviour of light and the nature of colour have been closely studied, but the results of the scientific research of Helmholtz and Ostwald—even the amateurish speculations of Goethe—are of little use to the æsthetician, who is concerned with colour as a factor of beauty, or to the layman, who cares very little what makes a tree green or a geranium red, but is immensely interested in the effect of colour on his emotional life.

The scientist can relate form to function more easily than he can relate colour to function. And even when he can prove, for example, that the hue of a flower is an important factor in its attractiveness to insects, he is working on too small a scale for his discoveries to be of real assistance to æsthetics. Moreover, his researches leave out of account the greater part of the layman's everyday experience of colour. The layman's colour experience of the world he lives in consists of various surfaces which possess the attribute of colour 'in their own right' or 'local' colour (which attribute depends on the molecular structure of the surface) modified by (*a*) the intensity of the light that illuminates them, and (*b*) the variation from whiteness of the light owing to interference between the source of light—the sun—which scientists agree to call 'white' and the illuminated object. These two 'conditions' of light, having nothing to do with molecular structure, are more easily and more quickly altered than 'local' colour. Nature constantly produces the same effects that in the theatre are produced by dimmers that reduce or increase the amount of light, or by coloured gelatines that alter its colour.

Every dawn and every dusk is an instance of a stepping up or dimming down of the amount of light. And the earth's atmosphere is a coloured gelatine that varies in its effect with every hour of the day, and can at sunrise and sunset produce the most violent disturbances, turning the sun crimson, graduating the normally blue sky from emerald green to gold and the normally white clouds from gold through pale rose to lilac. Even at midday the chromatic interference of a moisture-laden atmosphere on distant objects (i.e. objects seen through a greater amount of atmosphere) is well enough known to need no description or explanation. It is these modifications that confuse the issue. They are not properties of the object itself, but of the conditions under which it is seen. And the artist—the specialist in 'seeing'—seems instinctively to have felt this separation between the intrinsic character of objects and their temporary appearance so strongly that not until the middle of the sixteenth century did he begin seriously to turn his attention to the possibilities of light, and not until the middle of the nineteenth did he study more than superficially the *apparent* as opposed to the *local* colour of objects. And even then the study of such phenomena was largely confined to Europe. Oriental art has consistently refused to take more than a perfunctory interest in the impact of light, or in any but 'inherent' colour.

Truth of colour was therefore a much later object of the artist's attention than truth of form. Before the sixteenth century the painter permitted himself to invent colour schemes that had far less relationship to his chromatic experience of Nature than his forms had to the observed shapes of the objects he represented.

It would therefore seem that our ideas of what colour relationships are beautiful and what are not are far less conditioned by direct experience of Nature than our ideas of beauty of form. But here I may be wrong. It may be that our attention to the phenomenon of *apparent* colour in Nature is so recent a growth that our æsthetic appetites for colour are at present in an extremely primitive stage. It is not many decades since the Impressionists, in attempting to portray truth of colour, began to paint pictures that seemed to contemporary eyes chromatically ugly. It is only since the last decades of the nineteenth century that the typical Impressionist colour schemes have produced such an effect on our colour appetites that we have begun to demand, in the name of beauty, a set of colour harmonies that were originally presented to us in the name of truth.

This reference to painting may seem an irrelevant digression in a chapter dealing with æsthetic appetites based on visual experience of Nature and a sense of beauty dependent on the recognition of natural law. But our knowledge of the laws that produce colour is so fragmentary, and the fact that the laws themselves are of two kinds unrelated to each other, makes the world of colour extremely difficult to discuss. The enjoyment of colour cannot easily be thought of as the intuitive understanding of an underlying mathematical system. For that reason one is compelled to turn to the artist to find evidence of *his* experience of colour as embodied in his picture. Naturally his picture is more than a mere account of his experience: it is an ordered intensification of it. None the less, the nature of his experience of the world lived in can be roughly deduced from the picture he painted.

Now, although man's experience of colour is quite evidently divided into two departments, a certain amount of overlapping of the two has always taken place. Even the primitives reluctantly acknowledged a certain amount of interference with local colour caused by the intervening air. Their distances, for example, are conventionally bluer than their foregrounds. But more violent interferences, such as occur at sunset or sunrise, were studiously avoided. Perhaps the first attempt seriously to tackle a major interference with normal colour is the sky, and to some extent the landscape, in Giovanni Bellini's 'Agony in the Garden' of about 1465. And a good many modern painters, though their eyes had been opened to the phenomenon of interference by the Impressionists, have deliberately stressed inherent at the expense of apparent colour.

The whole question belongs, of course, to a later stage in this enquiry, but this brief digression is necessary here if only to suggest that colour-experience is in some way, in its very nature, different from form-experience. Scientifically speaking, the difference is between passive and active experience. For the apprehension of form depends on an active exploration by the eye which actually *moves* as it follows contour or passes across the surface of an object, accumulating and correlating images. Whereas colour is a mere sensation—a submission of the retina to a perpetual bombardment of light rays of various wave-lengths. This may seem, for practical purposes, a very slight difference, but in fact it is of the first importance. The education of the senses, like the education of every other faculty, is likely to be more complete and lasting if the pupil has taken an active part in his own education. The apprehension of form is the result of an effort: the apprehension of colour the result of nothing more than the sensibility of the retinal nerves. Form has to be read as one reads a book: colour can only be experienced as one experiences a hot bath. It is not an accident that makes it possible to speak of warm or cool colours. The same kind of vocabulary could not be applied to shape. There is a difference be-tween 'looking', which implies attentiveness, and 'seeing', which is no more than a sensation of the optic nerve. One *looks at* form: one *sees* colour. Attentiveness plays little or no part in our enjoyment of it.

For these reasons our feeling for beauty in colour is more sensuous and less intellectual than our feeling for beauty in form. Fewer dis-agreements arise, and a set of absolute æsthetic values is more easily arrived at. The *kind* of colour sensation that satisfies the normal human eye may be based to some extent on the kind of colour sensations that normally greet the eye in Nature—the balance between the areas of blue sky, green fields, white and grey clouds and so on: but it also depends on the mechanism of the eye itself, the amount of stimulus received by the nerves of the retina, and the amount of fatigue to which they are subjected.

Physiologists appear to argue that colour sensations are communicated to the brain by the innumerable nerve endings of the retinal nerve, which are arranged in groups—each group sensitive to a different set of wavelengths, which it 'translates' into colour sensations. Each group can be stimulated by the colour to which it is sensitive and can communicate æsthetic pleasure by means of it; it can also be fatigued and can therefore communicate æsthetic discomfort, by being subjected to unduly prolonged or unduly intense sensations.

It is not a question of brightness but of harmony, and many attempts have been made to establish laws of chromatic harmony. Most of them have been both tedious and inadequate, as indeed they were bound to be, for the simpler laws, based on the contrast of complementary colours and the relationship of primary to secondary colours, can be stated in a few words, while the complexity that occurs in Nature at almost every turn is far beyond analysis, since so many factors are involved. Relative luminosities, to which I shall return in a moment; relative tones—the contrast of light with dark; relative brilliancies—the contrast of bright and dull; relative areas—the contrast of small with large; juxtaposition—the distance between areas, all play their part. And, as with the mathematics of form, so with the physiology of colour, it is easy to lay down general principles but impossible to work them out in practical detail. Again, only the intuition can grasp such relationships. The curious may derive a little mild amusement from perusing the laborious list of contrasts and harmonies tabulated by Chevreuil (*The Principles of Harmony and Contrast of Colours*), but only the pedant could find them useful.

Attracted by the knowledge that colour sensations, like sound sensations, are the result of the impact of measurable wavelengths, theorists have attempted to formulate laws of chromatic harmony based on mathematics. But to work out a set of laws of harmony at all comparable to the laws of musical harmony has always proved impracticable since the musician is only concerned with a continuous single sequence of relationships; whereas our visual experience exists in space, and the time sequence is replaced by an area, every portion of which is seen simultaneously. Under such conditions the only laws that can be formulated are those imposed by the inherent nature of colour itself.

The simplest of these laws was hinted at just now, when I referred to the relative luminosities of colour. One of the most remarkable features of what is called "fully saturated colour"—colour that is at its maximum of purity, neither lightened by the addition of white nor darkened by the addition of black—is that each one has its own standard of luminosity. Looking at a spectrum, where all the colours are fully saturated, one is immediately conscious of a climax—a climax not of brilliance of hue but of brightness of light—somewhere about the centre, where the yellows and yellowish greens reside, and of a diminishing scale of brightness towards the blues on one side and the reds on the other. It is possible for the artist to interfere with this natural climax, to juxtapose a dark yellow with a pale blue, but he does so at his peril, just as a composer introduces a cacophony of sound at his peril. Nature herself indulges frequently in such cacophonies and only manages to conceal the fact that she is giving pain to the eye by the process, which I shall refer to later, of giving pleasure to the mind.

I had often suspected that this might be so, and a striking proof of it occurred some time ago when I was looking at a set of colour transparencies in a photographic exhibition. Thrown on to a screen in a dark room, these colour photographs were surprisingly "true to Nature" in their chromatic values, and I found that I could at will regard them either as actual views seen through the windows of a darkened room or as painted pictures hung against a black wall. In almost every case these flaming sunsets, sunlit gardens crowded with delphiniums and poppies, children in pink jumpers playing with emerald-green balls on golden sands, seemed enchanting when thought of as actual '*trompe l'œil*' scenes, and disgustingly tasteless and discordant when thought of as painted pictures. Occasionally—especially in her quieter twilit moods—Nature produced a good colour scheme rather like a Whistler nocturne, but her lapses into good taste were unbelievably rare. This process of adding or subtracting at will all the associations that lie behind the spectacle of Nature is not easily achieved under normal conditions. Here, by sheer chance, were provided the laboratory conditions under which it could be done. One could either participate in the moving pageantry of a sunset by 'watching' it, or one could see it objectively as an essay in colour-and-form arrangement. The difference between the two was unexpectedly disturbing.

Even apart from her disregard of colour harmony, there is a decided lack of colour balance in Nature. On the whole, she is timid in her use of the warm end of the spectrum. The preponderance of green, blue and grey (vegetation, sky and cloud) over red, yellow and orange, which are usually limited to minute areas such as flowers, berries and the smaller animals, is remarkable, and artists instinctively redress the balance. A range of colour harmonies which would be exotic and unfamiliar in Nature are a commonplace in art.

All this is discouraging evidence on which to base a theory that our standards of visual beauty are based on appetites engendered by our visual experience. At the opening of this chapter, I stated with some conviction that we cannot criticise Nature, since, being part of Nature, we have no outside standards wherewith to judge it. And yet here is an important department of natural phenomena which *can* be criticised. There can be only one reason for this breakdown of what I once regarded as an axiom—namely, that in regard to colour a standard of beauty *does* exist independent of the world of phenomena, a standard for which the key lies in the mechanism of the eye itself.

Clerk-Maxwell (in a lecture to the Royal Society) hinted at this when he said, "It seems almost a truism to say that colour is a sensation. . . . Some enquirers have supposed that they ought to study the properties of pigments: others that they ought to analyse the rays of light. They have sought for a knowledge of colour by examining something in external nature—something outside themselves. Now if the sensation we call colour has any laws, it must be something in our own nature that determines these laws." And yet in another place he argues that the mathematics of wave frequencies can have nothing to do with these laws because no mechanism for counting could possibly distinguish between such astronomical frequencies as 447 billion per second, which are seen as red, or the 570 billion that produce the sensation of green. But surely if the verb 'to count' means anything, it means to translate a number into a symbol, and a chromatic sensation is as valid a symbol as an arabic figure. If the retinal nerves could not 'count' frequencies, they would be unable to distinguish the frequencies that produce what we call 'green' from those we call 'red'.

Every consideration forces us to the conclusion that the world of colour, as we know it, is not only produced on a differently constructed chain of cause and effect from the world of form, but that our own apprehension of it is different in kind. The difference is rather like that between an alphabet and a dictionary. From a dictionary we can extract and arrange words and establish relationships between them, since each word carries with it its own little burden of meaning. And by an intelligent use of the dictionary we ourselves, if we have a 'meaning' to express, can produce literature. In fact, only through our knowledge of the dictionary can we develop a sense of what is, or is not, appropriate in literature.

But the colours we see around us, like the letters of the alphabet, are *not* charged with meaning. Like letters, they can be arranged in groups, and only when that has been done can they acquire a meaning.

Now Nature provides no counterpart to the colour-alphabet—unless it be the rainbow, which presents itself too rarely to be used as a standard work of reference. This alphabet is not part of everyday experience. An alphabet consists of a set of abstract concepts, and its true counterpart in the visual world is the paint-box. Given a paint-box, a hypothetical artist shut up from birth in a hypothetical prison could still evolve a world of colour, but he could not evolve a world of form. The concepts 'green' or 'red' would present no more difficulty to him than the concepts 'a' and 'b' to an illiterate child: but the concepts 'leaf' or 'geranium' could never be satisfactorily explained. Therefore our hypothetical artist, searching for 'beauty' of colour, would only have to experiment with his paint-box until he achieved a pleasurable sensation. He could never discover beauty of form by such a means.

Another analogy could be made with the world of sound. Nature provides a constant succession of sounds which, apart from rare exceptions—like the cuckoo's call—are not strictly musical, though they are received by the same mechanism as musical sounds in the form of wavelengths acting on the ear. Again, we are concerned with a set of sensations, a bombardment of wavelengths: and again we derive no standard of musical beauty from Nature. When we hear the wind in the trees or the snapping of a twig, we are subjected to a chaotic mixture of wavelengths like a chaotic mixture of letters of the alphabet. It is only when we have constructed a musical instrument— the audible equivalent of the paint-box—that we can begin to experiment with musical relationships and evolve from our experiments a set of appetites that will give us our standard of beauty.

CHAPTER III

Association

A MEADOW OF LUSH GRASS GENEROUSLY INTERSPERSED WITH buttercups and ox-eye daisies usually strikes one as beautiful. But what if on entering the meadow one were to discover that the buttercups were empty Gold Flake packets and the daisies torn up scraps of paper? One would protest to oneself in vain that litter and wild flowers can be equally pleasing to the eye, but despite one's attempts to preserve one's æsthetic judgments intact, one's attitude to the meadow would alter and the alteration could only be expressed in terms of disappointment. The eye cannot arbitrate alone. Each of our senses contributes its share to the total of sensation and perception, and what results is an amalgam far more complex than is commonly realised. The blackbird's song has an admirable purity, but its rhythm and its intervals are too elementary to be musically interesting. Yet, associated as it is with spring afternoons, sunshine and shady lawns, it becomes part of a sum of experiences, and it is a sufficiently important item in that sum to trap one into regarding it as exceptionally beautiful. The nightingale, musically rather less interesting than the blackbird, has gathered round itself so massive an accumulation of romantic associations with summer nights and moonlight that it is impossible to isolate it from its emotional context.

There is no such thing as a 'pure' experience. There may be a central experience, but the central experience is always either reinforced or contradicted by subsidiary experiences associated with it. And in daily life, in which all our senses are equally alert to sensations received from the outside world, the resultant total has a richness and complexity beyond the reach of analysis. In our experience of art, which by its very nature seeks to isolate sensation by addressing itself to one or two of the senses only, the amalgam is less complex, but it is still far from 'pure'. A symphony can never address itself to the ear alone. The architecture of the concert hall, the intensity and colour of the light, the condition and temperature of the atmosphere, the comfort or otherwise of the chair one sits on, all make their small additions to or subtractions from the central experience. The organisation of pure sound, intended by the composer for the ear alone, is no more than the most important item in an elaborate event; even if the symphony were performed in the dark, the senses of touch and smell would still operate, not to mention the ear itself which is continually assailed by sounds—coughs and shufflings of feet and rustlings of programmes— that were no part of the composer's intention and which have to be 'turned out' by the mental process of *listening*, although they cannot be eliminated from the mechanical process of *hearing*.

But the artist's attempt to isolate and purify our sensations is not yet in question. What must concern us now is our experience of life, in which no such attempt is being made—in which the word 'attempt' is irrelevant since it implies a purpose, and no one has yet divined the purpose of life. However inconvenient it may be to have to admit that the sense of sight is only one factor in our final estimate of what is visually beautiful, there is nothing to be gained by denying it. As long as visual beauty is regarded as a sensation produced by the mathe- matical behaviour of the visible world, the examination of beauty must confine itself to a rather dreary kind of mathematical analysis in which one thing is only more beautiful than another because it obeys a more complex or a more interesting mathematical formula than another.

Such an examination may explain one's conviction that a lupin leaf is more beautiful than a nasturtium or that the Matterhorn is more beautiful than Mount Etna, but it does not entirely answer the question raised in an earlier chapter, "Why is a horse more beautiful than a pig?" Certainly the horse's shape is more complex and therefore more interesting than the pig's, but not sufficiently so to account for the difference in our sense of their relative attractiveness.

The fundamental fact about organic nature is that it is functional. That is a short way of saying that given certain desires and fears and given a fixed environment, the plant or animal will inevitably so adapt and alter itself that it can most effectively gratify its desires and mini- mise its fears. Having eventually evolved the necessary adaptations and

55

alterations, it ceases to change and becomes a 'species'. After which only a change in the environment can provoke an alteration in the species. Each species is the final solution of a specific problem. And in particular the outward form of the species comes to be associated in our minds with its own problem. The length of the ant-eater's nose, the speed and length of its tongue, are a result of its appetite for ants: the length and strength of the gazelle's legs are the result of its fear of carnivores. Snouts become a symbol of greed, legs of speed.

There is no reason to suppose that any other force than the purely functional has been at work in the process of evolution. If Nature produces 'beauty', it is certainly not because beauty is *intrinsically* desirable, but because it has in some way proved useful to the species. What we call the beauty of the peacock or the passion flower must be a quality without which the peacock and the passion flower could not effectively fulfil their functions. And even if the beauty of the peacock is a product of a desire for beauty on the part of the peahen, it is certainly not a product of *man's* appetite for beauty. There is no reason to suppose that the peahen finds the peacock more desirable than the sow finds the boar. Nor is there any reason to suppose that the peahen finds the peacock's raucous voice less attractive than the gorgeous pattern of its tail or the brilliant sheen of its neck.

But if man's division of the world he lives in into more and less beautiful has nothing to do with the mechanism of evolution, it may easily have something to do with the sense of what functions are admirable or desirable. If he thinks the horse more beautiful than the pig (a verdict with which no pig could be expected to agree), the reason must be found in his feeling that the horse's desires and fears are somehow more sympathetic to him than the pig's: and that therefore the outward form and behaviour which are the visible symbols of those desires and fears are more acceptable. In other words, consciously or unconsciously, he has arranged functions in an order of merit of his own, based on their similarity to his own fears, desires and disgusts.

High on his list of desires is a desire for strength and speed, and in the horse's shape, no less than in its movements (which again have the rhythmic, mathematical basis without which there can be no beauty), he recognises a machine capable of more strength and power than he can develop himself. When he wishes to suggest even greater speed, he invents Pegasus, the winged horse. And when he wishes to ennoble himself and remove himself from contact with the gross earth, he endows himself with wings and invents the angel. High on his list of disgusts is a disgust of mud and dirt and of closeness to the earth, which the pig evidently does not share. These associations alone (and they are by no means the only ones) are sufficient, in combination with the purely visual perceptions of shape and colour, to give the horse an advantage over the pig, provided that the sum of perceptions and not merely the visual aspect of the two animals is taken into account. To the artist, and especially to the sculptor, for whom the visual experience is predominant, association necessarily plays a smaller, though never a negligible, part in the sum. I can imagine a sculptor refusing to admit that the pig as an arrangement of shape and mass is less pleasing than the horse. When we compare the horse with a table and the pig with a chest of drawers, the similarity of proportion and general design remains, but the similarity of function disappears; association ceases to play the same rôle: and with it the sense that the one is more admirable, and *therefore* more beautiful, than the other vanishes.

Once it has been admitted that though all Nature is equally functional, not all functions are equally admirable, we are confronted with a formidable rival, or, at least, a massive adjunct, to the mathematical theory of beauty. The beauty of the film star becomes a product of her desirability as well as of her symmetry, and her desirability can only be assessed by all the senses operating together to arrive at a combined verdict. The remarkable feature in this process is the power of the mind to arrive at a verdict without being conscious that the evidence on which it is based comes from so many different sources. It is remarkable enough that the mind can combine the separate visual images from our two eyes into a single stereoscopic image without being conscious that it is doing so. But to combine this visual image with perceptions independently provided by the other senses into a single emotional attitude is surely an extraordinary and an extremely convenient device. No conscious effort is involved. What does require a conscious effort is to disentangle all the heterogeneous ingredients that fuse together in a single emotional attitude.

In the case of everyday life the attempt is not worth making. Even if it could be done, it would serve no useful purpose. It is unprofitable to point out that the little pine woods near Martigues in France are no lovelier to the eye than those near Haslemere in Surrey, but that their delicious scent on a hot afternoon is one among the many factors that make them seem so. It is sufficient merely to note that beauty in Nature resides not only in the eye of the beholder but in his nose, his ears and his finger-tips. But the case of the arts is different. A work of art is a deliberate attempt on the part of the artist to produce the same emotional attitude by addressing himself to a limited set of sense perceptions. And the more limited the artist's appeal, the 'purer' one feels is his art. Instinctively we give to painting and sculpture, addressed only to the eye, and music, addressed only to the ear, a more honourable place in the hierarchy of the arts than to drama and opera which address themselves to both.

When therefore we find that violently divergent opinions exist as to the relative beauty of works of art that are ostensibly addressed to the eye alone, it is surely worth while to attempt to disentangle and classify the various factors that have led to these opinions.

Painting and sculpture, like music, certainly have their set of 'pure' or mathematical beauties, but unlike music they have a representational element which binds them to the *specific* experiences of life itself. No painting of a crucifixion, no painting of an apple, can be thought of as no more than a piece of formal planning. Once the figure of Christ or the apple has been recognised, the door stands open and a flood of association pours in. These associations may combine with and enhance the picture's 'beauty' or they may detract from it. But they cannot fail to affect it. And the less sensitive the spectator to formal beauty, the more association will weigh with him in his final assessment.

CHAPTER IV

Art

EXPERIENCE ALONE CAN FERTILISE THE WOMB IN WHICH A WORK
of art is conceived. What is called the artist's imagination—
the part of his creative mechanism responsible for envisaging
the work of art, as opposed to creating it—is merely a machine in
which his experience of life is sorted out and dealt with. Some of his
experiences he rejects as being useless to him, others he cherishes as
being particularly precious. When, at last, he arrogates to himself the
powers of a god and turns his conceptions into works of art, his creations may be hardly recognisable as records of experience, just as a
string of sorted pearls may be only dimly reminiscent of an oyster-
bed or a bottle of brandy of a vineyard. It is astonishing to discover
how impressively the great imaginative artists of the world have
managed to use the commonplaces of human experience. What they
have achieved has been done, not by the invention of new forms, but
by the distillation, the intensification of familiar ones. The memorable
gestures of Michelangelo's athletes, the glowing distances of Claude's
landscapes, the gradations of light on which Rembrandt dwells, are
all part of every man's visual experience. Yet by sorting out and
isolating these commonplaces and by rejecting everything irrelevant
to them, each of these men gives the impression of having created a
new world.

Blake's stock of images—the visual vocabulary at his disposal—was
absurdly small; indeed, it consists largely of clichés and borrowings;
but with it he worked miracles. The artist may appear to have created
something so full of his own dæmon that it achieves a self-contained
existence of its own and seems to reveal an inner life that is almost
independent of the outer world. None the less, just as the oyster-bed
is the true parent of the necklace, so experience of life is the true parent

59

of the work of art. The inner life is a by-product of the outer world. And that applies not merely in the narrow sense that is obviously true of works of representational art; it is equally true of buildings and chairs, or of symphonies and perfumes which represent nothing in particular. Ideas of rigidity and flexibility, of straightness and curvature, of simplicity and complexity, of hardness and softness, without which no chair could be envisaged, such ideas can only be engendered in the chair-designer's mind by their counterparts in Nature.

It is true, then, to say that the work of art is a child whose mother is the artist and whose father is the artist's environment. In that sense we, the consumers and enjoyers of art, are uncles and aunts to the work of art. We have taken no part in their creation, yet they belong to our family. Our parents are their grandparents. The artists who made them are our sisters and brothers.

This puts us in a special relationship to all works of art. Our attitude to a tree is bound to be quite different from our attitude to a picture by Titian. The tree was fashioned by the same forces that fashioned us. The Titian was fashioned by someone rather like ourselves, using the same *kind* of raw material that is available to us too. But Titian is not identical with ourselves, and his raw material is not identical with ours. The set of personal preferences that guided his sorting process is not the same as ours. Given the same oyster-bed, our necklace of pearls would have been different from Titian's. We therefore have the right to criticise the Titian, whereas we have no right to criticise the tree. We may admire the Titian. We may be forced to acknowledge that his sorting process shows far more sensitiveness and discernment than we are capable of ourselves. But, though we may be his inferiors in imaginative power, we are his equals in status.

It follows therefore that what we call the beauty of a Titian is different in kind from the beauty of a tree. The latter we have no choice but to accept: it is from the tree itself that we derive our notion of beauty in trees. The former we need not accept at all unless it satisfies a hunger we have already developed for beauty in works of art. And the nature of that hunger is bound to depend on our preconceived ideas about works of art. And since Titian, as already mentioned, was rather like ourselves—a European who had absorbed very much the same kind of culture and civilisation as ourselves—the probability is that we shall find his picture beautiful. Our preconceptions will be, at least collaterally, related to his own.

Moreover, it must be remembered that Titian's experience of life, the storehouse from which he sorts out the ingredients for his picture, includes his experience of other works of art. He is just as intimately familiar with the pictures of his master, Giovanni Bellini, and of his contemporary Giorgione, as he is with trees. In stringing *his* necklace of pearls, he has before him examples of other men's attempts at pearl-stringing. And though none of their necklaces will seem to him to be strung quite as he would have strung them himself, yet they are bound to influence him.

We, too, the consumers of art, have had our appetites for beauty conditioned and modified by our knowledge of works of art. Our experience of life, too, is not confined to natural phenomena. Even more than Titian himself are we conscious of the artist's creations, for our experience includes works Titian never dreamed of, works done since Titian died. And each of those works has contributed to the shaping of our æsthetic appetites, and thereby altered our sense of beauty.

Now just as our acceptance of an oyster-bed depends on our recognition that it forms part of the harmonious ensemble of life, so our acceptance of the string of pearls depends on our recognition of its relationship to the oyster-bed. If the beholder's mind fails to grasp that relationship—if the string of pearls is so strange and unfamiliar that no conceivable process of sorting, isolating, rejecting and arranging will account for it—at once the work of art becomes unintelligible and therefore ugly. Nothing in our experience has prepared us for that particular manifestation of the human imagination. No appetite for that particular form of visual diet exists in us. Therefore we reject it. And we rationalise our rejection by the simple process of calling it ugly. That happens rarely in the case of the old—even the oldest—masters. If it did, only two explanations would be possible. Either the artist in question had wasted his time in sorting out particularly worthless pearls, and ours by presenting them to us: or his feeling for pearls was so very unlike our own that his necklace is unacceptable to us.

I can imagine, for example, a native of West Africa confronted by his first Monet, or a seventeenth-century Dutchman confronted with his first Sung landscape, rejecting them utterly as being unrelated to his experience. His oysters had never produced anything as queer as that: therefore they cannot possibly be pearls. But, on the whole, the old masters carry their birth certificates with them. A little thought, a little comparison between them and others like them, will convince most people that they all had a reasonable method of sorting out from the rag-bag of experience just what they needed. What they needed was, perhaps, different from what we need, but we find it easy enough to make allowances for the change that time brings about.

But with our own contemporaries the case is different. Their experience is almost identical with our own. They, like ourselves, know all about aeroplanes and telephones and mass-production and Communism. Like us, they have absorbed the second-hand experience of life passed on to them and to us by artists of the past. But they have their own experiences to sort out and arrange, and, like each of their predecessors, they have their own individual ways of doing it. New combinations occur to them which had never occurred to any previous artist. So that when we are confronted with their works of art we are looking at something unfamiliar, something that is not yet a part of our experience. Our instinctive reaction is to reject it in proportion to its unfamiliarity. And if the artist in question has chosen to select and isolate a type of experience that has never been dealt with before, it is almost impossible not to reject it utterly. He is giving us a diet for which we are unprepared. We do not stop to ask whether we are behaving rationally, for appetite is never rational. We mentally transfer our incapacity to understand this new manifestation of the human spirit to the artist who created it. We put the blame on him, and we condense our failure to understand into one word—'ugly'. What we mean is "unintelligible to me as an account of another man's experience". The word 'ugly' can mean nothing else as applied to a work of art. Applied to a tree, it would mean something different. It would mean "unintelligible to me as an instance of the law-abiding behaviour of natural phenomena".

But that word 'ugly', usually uttered with a tinge of exasperation that an artist should have had the effrontery to present us with something so unpalatable, somehow lacks assurance. It has none of the air of finality when it is applied to art that it has when we use it about Nature. There is no hostility in our tone of voice when we apply it to a pig or to an octopus. We are angry neither with the pig nor with the pig's Maker. But our exasperation with the artist who refuses to do his job as we would like him to, or as artists of the past have taught us to expect him to, is a weakness, and we know it. We suspect—quite rightly—that the next generation will not be hostile, for they will understand what we cannot understand. They will understand the artist's intention, for it will have been part of their familiar environment. They may not think it a very important or significant intention, or they may find it quite fascinating. In the first case they will call his work of art 'mediocre', in the second 'beautiful'. But only rarely will they call it ugly. And when they do, they will use the word dispassionately.

If, then, the word 'beauty' can shift its whole direction in the course of a couple of decades, it is surely worth examining the nature of these man-made phenomena, these works of art, which, without undergoing the slightest change in themselves, are capable of arousing hostility in one generation and admiration in the next. Our main enquiry must be into the strange fluctuations of what is known as 'taste', the power to distinguish between degrees of beauty and between kinds of beauty in art. But before doing so, it will be necessary to find out what art itself is made of.

I am not concerned here with the artist's motive in creating his work of art. I am content to take him for granted, I am willing to ignore him altogether except as a womb in which art is conceived, just as I am willing to ignore God altogether except as an originator of matter and an inventor of the laws that govern the behaviour of matter. The 'why?' and the 'whither?' of God and man, of Nature and art, are questions for the philosopher. My concern is with the 'what?'

At this point, as soon as we begin to examine art more closely, my pearl-necklace analogy will no longer serve. It wormed its way into the last few paragraphs against my will. Like all analogies, it breaks down on close inspection. Art is far more than a selection of scraps that seem particularly attractive to the artist, chosen from a bewilderingly large rag-bag and arranged in a way that seems to him particularly desirable. Such an image is useful enough for the purpose of distinguishing between Nature, the big central warehouse, and art, the little, specialised retail shop. But once that broad distinction has been made, art must submit herself to a closer analysis.

Closer analysis reveals her to be something far more complicated in structure than Nature. Unlike Nature, she turns out to be full of human intentions, points of view, comments, boredoms, preferences, all of which must be understood if art is to be understood. Nature, for all her inexhaustible variety, is, as it were, all on one level, a limit-less, two-dimensional area of which man has hitherto explored only one fragment. She can be compared to the foundation on which the house of art is built, or, better, to the axioms and postulates upon which a Euclid constructs his propositions. Euclid's "a straight line is the shortest distance between two points" could be paralleled by saying, "An oak tree is the shortest distance between two generations of acorns". That, presumably, is Nature's view of an oak tree—a purely functional view. The artist's view is different. To him an oak tree is far more than a machine for producing acorns. It can be a symbol of strength, an arrangement of masses, a colour scheme in dark brown and yellowish green, a stimulus to his sense of curvature or his sense of proportion. It can give rise to a host of attitudes of mind, each or all of which can contribute to a work of art. If Nature is two-dimensional, art is three-dimensional, full of different levels, an onion rather than a plain, a thing that can be held in the hand, but which will never reveal its secrets unless one realises that its outer visible skin is almost nothing. The skin must be peeled off, and under the skin, layer after layer must be peeled off in turn until, right in the centre of it, a hard core is discovered, a core that has something to do with the mysteries of the human soul.

What interests me is the structure of this onion. Hundreds of thoughtful, sensitive men have made it their business to examine some particular layer of it. The weakness of almost all their thought and sensitivity lies in a tendency to seize on one particular layer and to assert that here and here only is the key to the mystery. But I can think of no writer whose central theme has been the close interlocking, the delicious fitting together of layer to layer, so that the whole becomes an integrated solid, a complex whole of which neither the skin nor the core can reveal the secret, but only the continuous texture that leads from one to the other and binds them together.

For convenience take the case of paintings. Not that for my purpose there is any essential difference between paintings and chairs, dramas, symphonies or epic poems. But a painting does offer a laboratory specimen of unusual completeness, for in it, as we shall see, the onion has an extra layer.

Here, then, is a picture, a flat surface of a certain size and of a well-defined shape, on to which the artist has spread certain pigments in such a way that they will convey certain intentions that once existed in his mind's eye and in *his* mind's eye alone, to our minds' eyes by way of our physical eye. The reader may possibly disagree with this definition of a picture, but it must stand for the moment. It is no more than a convenient nail to hang our onion from while we examine its structure.

The majority of paintings are representational. The artist, that is to say, has so spread his pigments on to his surface that they remind us of objects known to us or intelligible to us because of our own experience of life. The picture has a subject. It 'represents' a landscape, a vase of flowers, a group of people, and in so far as it does so our first reaction to it is one of recognition. We refer the landscape, the flowers or the people in the picture back to our own memories of landscapes, flowers or people. We compare these recognisable forms with our own memories of such forms, and we are, on the whole, pleased if the pictured forms confirm our memories and displeased if they do not. This is the onion's outer skin. The artist has not yet begun to speak with his own voice. His function on this outermost level of painting differs in no respect from that of the camera. He is merely describing appearances; translating, as the camera does, the volumes of Nature into two-dimensional terms. I do not know what percentage of beholders never succeed in peeling off this outer skin, but I suspect that it is rather large. "It is in execrable taste, having no resemblance to any appearance in Nature" (*Gentleman's Magazine* on Constable's 'Hadleigh Castle', 1829) is the kind of criticism which can only be made by persons who refuse to penetrate the outer skin.

It is quite a different attitude from that of the critic who recognises the artist's representational or descriptive skill but considers it misplaced or misused. "It is badly drawn, badly coloured and, what is much worse, indelicate. Why are the modest and lovely young females who daily grace the rooms of Somerset House with their presence, to have their feelings outraged and blushes called into their cheeks by a work like this?" (*Literary Gazette* on James Ward's 'Venus Rising from her Couch', 1830). Here the critic dislikes the skin but is not content to stop there: he peels it off and finds the next layer unpalatable.

James Ward, Diana and Her Nymphs
Roland, Browse & Delbanco's Gallery, London

66

Constable, Hadleigh Castle
National Gallery, London

It is on this next layer that the artist begins to speak for himself. As a recorder of appearances, he can only be admired for his skill and accuracy, or blamed for his lack of them. On the inner levels he begins to assert his attitude to life. Praise and blame for what he has done take on a different note—the note in which one man speaks of another's intentions and judges him by a set of values of his own. The critic of the *Literary Gazette* complains that James Ward's Venus is "badly drawn and badly coloured", by which I assume him to mean that James Ward has to some extent failed to paint his Venus with an outline or in colours that accurately represent a real live woman. But he regards the artist's failure to represent Venus convincingly in paint as much less important than his success in representing her in such a way that she will bring a blush to the cheeks of lovely young females. This is not the place to enquire closely into the attitude of the 1830s towards the nude in painting, or to ask why the writer should have chosen to be indignant on behalf of the 'lovely' as well as the 'modest'.

Such an enquiry comes under the heading of 'taste', and must be reserved for a later chapter. The point now at issue is that the critic himself distinguishes between bad drawing, which is a question of skill, and 'indelicacy', which is a question of an attitude of mind. In the layer below the outer skin, therefore, the artist expresses his attitude to his subject-matter. He comments on it, and in doing so he does something that the camera cannot do. He is painting, say, a plateful of apples: as he looks at the apples a set of preferences begins to form itself in his mind's eye. The apples are green and shiny and round, but he cannot be equally interested in all three aspects of them. One or other of those aspects begins to dominate his attitude to the apples. Fascinated by their greenness, he begins to forget about their texture and their volume. From all other possible qualities that belong to these particular apples, he isolates the quality of greenness. He modifies the colour of his background so that their greenness shall be intensified by the juxtaposition. He eliminates the highlight that would express their shininess because it would detract from their colour; he suppresses the shadow they cast and the modulations of tone at their edges so as not to insist too much on their solidity. He has expressed his attitude of mind towards those particular apples. He has made his personal comment.

But it is a comment too closely tied up with his subject-matter to allow him much freedom of personal expression. That layer can be peeled off easily enough. Below it is something more important and more personal, namely the artist's attitude to the visible world in general. There is, perhaps, little essential difference between this layer and the last, but in it the artist begins to speak of his own preferences with more authority and to break away from the domination of his subject-matter. It is on this level that he deals most ruthlessly with his experience. He pursues passionately those aspects of the visible world which excite him, and in the eagerness of his pursuit he tends to link up with others of his kind and to form groups or schools of artists with a common generic set of excitements. The physical eye looking out at the world admits everything and selects nothing, but the messages it sends along the sensory nerves are submitted in the brain to a system of sifting and sorting that colours the artist's 'style'. The Persian rejects practically all visual messages that cannot be converted into pattern; the Florentine sorts out those which explain structure; the Impressionist ignores whatever is not related to light and atmosphere. All of them take on the unmistakable tone that distinguishes the lover from the scientist. "This is what I have seen" gives place to "This is what I have loved". Blindness, the lover's proverbial prerogative, contributes just as much as vision to the final result. The Persian *must* be blind to shadow and perspective; the Florentine to the atmospheric envelope that enfolds the world; the Impressionist to those delicate modulations of line which captivated the artists of the early Renaissance. Only by this combination of love and blindness can the artist speak with full effect. To the scientist a rose is a rose; to the artist it may be an intricate pattern like a snowflake, or a formless blur of pink like a bursting rocket, or an assemblage of minute curved surfaces that catch and reflect and absorb the light like the cut surfaces of a diamond. It is essential that each of these interpretations—these lover-like attitudes of mind—should be expressions of the truth. It is equally essential that they should not be the whole truth. But what is characteristic of them all is that they reveal the artist's love, not of roses but of the visible world in general. A pair of boots or a mountain would serve his purpose equally well. And with that one may as well dismiss what is, I am convinced, the thickest, the most richly flavoured layer of the onion.

Beneath it lies a layer that is less definable, in which the gradual process, which the reader will doubtless have noted, of breaking away from subject-matter is now complete. I hesitate to call it the level of pure æsthetics, for the word has a pedantic ring. But no other word exists for what the artist is getting at now. He is no longer concerned with apples or roses or human beings, but only with shapes and colours, with proportions and contrasts and juxtapositions. On the face of it these preoccupations may seem a little inhuman, and yet it is here that the lover ceases to speak and begins to sing. The praises of his beloved are no longer mere statements governed by his vision or his blindness. They become rhythmic, like psalms, and as little connected with representation as music. We are getting near to the core of the onion. On this level the arts meet. The painter is doing what the builder of a cathedral or the designer of a ballet or the composer of a nocturne is doing. All these men are putting together the kinds of shapes and colours, or of movements or sounds, that please them. They are still closely linked up with their experience of life, still sorting titbits out of the general storehouse, but not in the same spirit as on the outer levels. A love of green apples is now a love of greenness, a love of oak trees is now a love of roughness and sturdiness. If the picture is filled with shapes and colours that are in themselves rough and sturdy, then the artist is neither describing an oak tree nor expressing his attitude to an oak tree. He is weaving a spell about oak-treeness.

There is something rather remote about spells. They insult the intellect because they ignore it. Their potency depends on their power to short-circuit straight from the point of reception—the eye, the ear, the finger-tips, the nose—to the seat of the emotions. Music can do this infallibly; no lover of music could tolerate a sound-pattern that failed to do it. Visual art must also do it, though the artist's obligation to bewitch as well as to describe and comment is less obvious. Because the artist *can* both describe and comment, his function as spellbinder is apt to be forgotten, buried under the outer layers of the onion. And yet, forgotten or not, it is always there. The curves of the drapery in a fresco by Giotto are curves as well as draperies; the line that encloses a foot or a hand in a picture by Botticelli is a thread that entangles the eye, as well as an account of the shape of a hand or foot. It means as much (or as little) as the curve that encloses the dome of St. Paul's or the wing of a Spitfire. These last are curves in their own right. Wren has an advantage over Botticelli, for no one confuses *his* curve with hands and feet. The architect's spell is not caught up and entangled, as the painter's is, with the fringes of the material world.

Among the painters of to-day there are a few who so resent this entanglement that they desperately try to become architects in their painting. By refusing to describe or comment, they bravely proclaim their abstract intentions in shapes and colours that 'mean' nothing; that are, in fact, nothing but two-dimensional architecture or visual music. There is logic on their side, but little else. "I am an artist," runs their argument. "My business is to arrange the shapes and colours that please me in a way that pleases me. Why therefore should I confuse myself with irrelevances—with draperies and trees and all the paraphernalia of the visible world? And, above all, why should I distract

the eye of the man who looks at my colours and shapes with unnecessary references to trees and draperies?"

He is right, this uncomfortable puritan. He is infuriatingly right,
like all logicians. The very heart of the problem is here, the organ that
pumps life-blood through the body of the picture. But in his hatred
of irrelevances he has forgotten one thing, namely that a heart by
itself is useless. A heart without a body is no more than a machine.
The more efficiently it works, the more pitiful it seems that there is no
work for it to do.

And now we are at the threshold of the ultimate mystery. Even in
imagination one hesitates to strip off this last layer; for what lies
within really is the core. Even if the human mind could grasp its
nature, the dictionary would still be unable to supply the words needed
to describe it. One must flounder, stammering, round it, groping
for metaphors, in the hope that some casual word will accidentally
illuminate it. No doubt the scientist would dearly love to vivisect
the body if he thought that by so doing he could isolate the soul
and hastily embalm it in technical terms before it disintegrated.
But the scientist knows well enough that his clumsy instruments
cannot perform the hazardous operation. He must leave it to the
lover; and the lover refuses the attempt, not because he knows it is
impracticable but because he feels it is impious. About this ultimate
core only two things can be said that have any meaning at all. First, it
is something that the artist himself knows nothing whatever about.
Second, it is the only part of the onion that is really concrete. The rest
belongs to the realm of the artist's eyesight or his imagination or his
æsthetic urge. But here at the very centre, where one would expect to
find oneself utterly free from the domination of tangible matter, is
something that surprisingly depends on sable-hair brushes and powdered earths and linseed-oil, on charred vine stems and hand-made
paper—stuff that can be purchased in the shop round the corner.
It is as though one had stumbled on the extraordinary discovery that
the body, far from housing the soul, is in reality housed by it, pro-
tected and encased and nourished by it. That it is the body and not
the soul that contains the final secret of life.

This innermost core is a kind of chemical fusion between the
artist's unconscious mind and his chosen medium. Each reacts on the

71

other as inevitably as the interaction of two chemicals. No matter what subject the artist may have chosen to depict, no matter what aspect of his experience he may have chosen to stress, choice is no longer his once he begins to practise his craft. His hand and the brush he holds in his hand move in obedience to impulses over which he has no control. Each stroke of the brush on the canvas, each scratch of the needle on the etcher's plate, expresses something that has no more to do with his painterly or draughtsmanly 'intentions' than a man's handwriting has to do with the meaning of the sentence he writes. In fact, if this innermost core is to be given a label, it may as well be called 'handwriting'. The word is inadequate. Though it points in the right direction, it is lamentably lacking in force. This fusion of unconscious impulse with conscious craftsmanship leaves an imprint on the picture far more definitive and significant than handwriting leaves on the sentence. It permeates the whole work with the artist's personality. And it shows itself in terms of the natural behaviour of his medium. When Titian is painting his picture, he is engaged without knowing it in fusing Titianness with paintness. For paint has a wilful, obstinate set of qualities and habits of its own which Titian can direct but can never alter; and Titian's brush obeys a set of inflexible impulses whose direction neither he nor his medium can deflect. How often have I listened patiently to a painter explaining precisely what he is aiming at in his picture: how he has tried to express this or that fine shade of emotional meaning, capture this or that overtone and find a means of translating it into paint. What he said was usually true, and the account of his struggle to externalise his vision was usually revealing. But the important thing he always left unsaid. He never mentioned that his wrist insisted on moving in a different tempo, with a different rhythm from any other painter's in the past or the future. 'Insisted' is the wrong word, for it implies an obstacle surmounted, a hurdle cleared. In this business of handwriting there is no obstacle. It is the painter's most precious possession, yet it is his easiest task. The path from his unconscious mind to the tip of his paint-brush is free from all obstruction. The nervous impulses travel along it as easily and inevitably as an electric current along a copper wire. Perhaps that image does, in fact, supply the spark of illumination for which this central core of art has been waiting. The electricity is the quintessence of the artist's self: the copper wire is his medium, his little blob of paint, his little stick of charred vine stem, that beckon him along the only channel open to him. It is that quintessence, combined with that beckoning, that gives to every artist his own, unmistakable flavour and determines the shape of the stylistic signature that every painter scrawls unwittingly across his whole canvas.

The layers of the onion can now be seen in relation to each other. They form a progression. On the level of the skin the artist is an observer; on the next level, that of the outer layer, he is a commentator; on the second layer he is an interpreter; on the third a visionary, and finally, when he reaches the core, a creator.

At each stage in the progression he leaves the tangible, visible world—the apple, or whatever it may be that he has chosen as his subject-matter—a little farther behind and explores the intangible, invisible world of his *vie intérieure*. Having explored it, he endeavours to find a visual symbol for it, and that symbol is the clue to his secret. Just as the ant-eater's snout is a symbol of his appetites and the gazelle's legs of his fear, so, in its deeper levels, the work of art is a symbol of the artist's appetites and fears, his final externalisation of himself as an individual.

As a recorder of the apple's outward appearance, the painter has no individuality. He is at the mercy of the apple and of his own eyesight, just as a thermometer is at the mercy of the temperature of the object with which it comes into contact and of the nature of mercury. But as soon as he begins to exercise his rights as an individual and to take up an attitude to the apple—to love its greenness or to be bored with its roundness—he has taken the first step on the road to creation. And at the third layer, when he is no longer concerned with concrete apples but with abstract greenness, he begins to acquire the attributes of a creator. At that point, beauty in the mathematical sense enters into his creation, though his is a different kind of mathematics from Nature's. All the qualities I have described as belonging to the third, the æsthetic, layer are expressible in terms of mathematics. The harmonies, proportions, contrasts, juxtapositions, curves are the pearls he has extracted from Nature's oyster because he had a passionate desire to discover them. And though it needed the original stimulus of the apple to initiate the desire, once it has been engendered the apple is no longer necessary. The pictured apple is now self-sufficient because it has discovered its own mathematical foundation. Like Nature, it is beautiful because it is obedient to law, but this time the law is its creator's sense of order and harmony. Briefly, the artist's attitude is, "This shape and no other is the shape I desire". Nature's attitude is, "This shape and no other is the shape that will work".

What forces have determined the quality and direction of the artist's desires is a question for the psychologist; just as what forces determined the laws of Nature is a question for the scientist. It is improbable that either question will ever be fully answered. Meanwhile, the art critic, who is concerned with effects rather than causes, can at least analyse the work of art even though its ultimate derivation remains a mystery.

And now, having peeled our onion, it remains for the analyst to put the layers back again, contemplate the onion once more as an integral whole, and to confess, rather shamefacedly, that it was never really an onion at all. It was no more an onion than it was a string of pearls. For, though it was arranged in layers exactly as I have described, the layers were never separate from each other. Its texture ran through from skin to core without a break, each layer melting imperceptibly into the next on the journey from the outer skin of objective description to the inner core of unconscious handwriting. The analyst may allow himself the licence of splitting the object of his researches into a set of arbitrary component parts, but having done so, he must confess that he was practising a harmless deception for the reader's convenience. Art can no more be thought of in terms of superimposed layers than water can be thought of as a mixture of hydrogen and oxygen, or a musical chord as a series of notes sounded in succession. The layers exist only in theory. In practice they interpenetrate each other so completely that in looking at a given work of art, the beholder is conscious of them all simultaneously, and is therefore not conscious of them at all.

CHAPTER V

The Medium

COLOURED POWDER MIXED WITH YOLK OF EGG, SPREAD BY means of animal's bristles on to a surface of smoothed plaster; ink transferred to paper from grooves bitten by nitric acid in a plate of polished copper—these are all that the eye sees when one looks at Piero della Francesca's 'Nativity' or Rembrandt's etching of 'The Crucifixion'. The unbroken chain of cause and effect that begins with the dreams and aspirations of men ends in powdered earth and printer's ink or in stretched catgut stroked by horsehair or felt-covered hammers beating on piano wire.

Only by the construction of this chain can a work of art come into being, and only by that impact of the printer's ink on his eye or the vibrating wire on his ear can the spectator or the listener reach back, link by link, along the chain till he arrives at the dream that was once conceived in the mind of Rembrandt or Beethoven. And if, as I am convinced, love begat the dream, then one is faced once more with this strange process whereby love, working its will through the artist, expresses itself, finally, in ridiculously measurable terms, and emerges as a set of light waves or sound waves, expressible in purely mathematical formulæ, operating in a purely mechanical way on the retinal nerve-ends or the ear-drum.

It is a familiar enough process despite its seeming absurdity. In fact it is the only process whereby communication can be made between one human being and another. Our only means of access to the universe we live in are our sensory nerves, and the only way in which the universe can affect them is through measurable vibrations. The lover expresses the infinite intensity of his longing for his beloved by converting it into sound waves, which the beloved converts once more into emotion by means of her ear-drum and the nerves which connect her ear-drum to her brain. But when the lover says, "I love you", he is producing a comparatively simple sequence of sound waves. When Rembrandt has finished saying what he has to say about the Crucifixion in terms of printer's ink distributed unevenly on a sheet of paper, he has created a set of light waves of far greater complexity.

The word 'medium', which does duty for this final material element in a work of art, is convenient but rather misleading. It is true that the printer's ink does mediate between Rembrandt's own private dream and our realisation of it. Without the ink and the paper we should have no means of knowing the quality of his dream. But the word must not be thought of as meaning that every line scratched on the plate by Rembrandt's needle is, as it were, a copy of a line already visualised in his mind's eye. To regard the movements of the artist's hand as the result of a series of commands from his creative mind is to over-simplify the process known as 'technique' and 'craftsmanship'.

Those commands certainly do operate the etcher's needle, but even while they are doing so the needle itself is sending messages back to the creative mind. The medium has a will of its own, a behaviour natural to it, which the artist must take into account. And the process of taking the will of the medium into account is the essence of crafts-manship. If he ignores the medium's natural behaviour and forces his own will on it, he does so at his peril: if he yields too easily, allowing it to dominate his will, that, too, he does at his peril. The secret of craftsmanship lies in exploiting the medium, making it subserve his will without forcing it into a behaviour unnatural to it. Like the Japanese wrestler who turns his opponent's effort to his own advantage and makes him assist in his own downfall, the artist amalgamates the medium's will with his own.

In order to do so he must be acutely sensitive to the messages that travel back to him from the needle's point—complaints about too much pressure, requests for more speed, hints that the grip of the fingers on the stem of the needle must be relaxed a little if the line is not to lose its flexibility. An endless series of conferences must take place in the artist's mind as these messages come pouring in and modify or are modified by the orders that go out. *This* portion of the line must be as rigid as a bar of steel; *here* the tension can relax and the needle can, if it wants to, glide carelessly over the copper surface like

Rembrandt, Crucifixion
The first and fourth states of etching
British Museum, London

cigarette smoke coiling through the air; *now* for the emphatic change of direction where the seductive sensation of the point sliding over the metal surface must at all costs be resisted.

In the case of Rembrandt's etching of 'The Crucifixion' we are in the fortunate position of being able to follow his changes of intention, as he worked, by studying the different 'states' of the plate. One sees, not only the process of elaboration, but of revision and even of major alteration. And it is not difficult, in comparing one 'state' with the next, to guess which modifications were suggested by his sense of the medium's possibilities and which by his deepening conception of the theme itself.

The medium dictates its own terms to the artist. Consequently it is not enough to regard him as a man with a dream who translates his dream into a mental image and then translates the image into visible terms. During the process of translation the dream itself suffers a change.

There is, of course, no possibility of defining the change. There is certainly a relationship between a mental image and its final translation into visual form. But the two can never be compared. It is not merely that they belong to different categories which by their very nature cannot be compared: but also the dream is the private property of the artist and its very existence can only be deduced from the existence of the translation. The two are related in the sense that the Platonic 'phenomenon' is related to the 'idea' of which it is a shadow. The artist himself 'knows' the precise nature of his dream, but his knowledge is of no avail to us since his communication of his knowledge to us can only take the form of a translation, and that translation *is* the work of art. He can attempt to express in words just how and to what extent he has failed to make the translation fit the dream, but his words themselves are merely another form of translation. We are cut off from his real life, his inner life, by the simple fact that he is an individual whose only hope of making emotional contact with other individuals is by the purely physical process of affecting their sensory nerves. The artist can do no more than trust that the messages they communicate to our minds will bear a rough similarity to the messages originally sent out by him while he was making his work of art. We, at the receiving end, are in the position of people condemned to communicate with our fellows by telephone only. The noises we hear cannot be compared with human voices, for we have never heard human voices. Therefore we cannot tell whether any defects we may find in them are due to the halting speech of the subscriber at the other end of the line or to the strange behaviour of the telephone itself.

The problem, however, is purely academic. To the philosopher it may be of some interest, but for the art critic it does not arise. His concern is not with the word that was spoken but with the word he has overheard. And half the fun of his job lies in comparing the quality of one telephone with another. The other half lies in making guesses about the nature of the 'distant subscriber'.

Manifestly this book, whose avowed object is to define the nature of beauty in art, must be largely concerned with the origin of the noises heard on our metaphorical telephone, but it cannot afford to ignore the nature and behaviour of the telephone itself. I do not propose to describe in detail the precise characterisation of each type of medium: there is an abundant literature on that subject. But it will be necessary at least to refer to the *kind* of modification which the chosen medium is likely to make on the artist's vision.

Certain artists are instantly recognisable as having 'exploited' their medium to the full. They are not necessarily the greatest, and many of them are second-rate artists who are content to use their art as a means of advertising their skill in handling their medium. But what differentiates them from the type of artist who is not primarily a great craftsman or technician is that they have been exceptionally sensitive and obedient to the messages conveyed to the mind by the medium itself. If they are great creative artists, like Velazquez or Rembrandt, the result is a magnificent collaboration between the medium's behaviour and the creative will. Where the creative will is weak or the vision mediocre but the handling masterly, the word 'slick' has been invented to express just that victory of 'handling' over vision that invariably results in a mediocre work of art. Between the two extremes are artists like Franz Hals, whose technical facility makes one suspect that the messages from his brush to his mind were more urgent than those operating in the reverse direction.

But though it is usually possible to guess, in the case of a given artist, just how sensitive he has been to the behaviour of his medium, to what extent he has taken advantage of its possibilities and to what extent he has ignored them, he can never ignore them entirely, because he is, by definition, a man who has expressed himself in terms of a *chosen* medium. And his only reason for choosing one medium rather than another is his sense that, for the purpose of what he has to express, the chosen medium is somehow more eloquent than all others. It is for the psychologist to discover why sound is eloquent to the musician, pigment to the painter, movement to the dancer. But the critic's job is to note how the mode of expression has, paradoxically, modified the flavour and even the very essence of the thing expressed.

Looking back at the history of media in the visual arts, it is evident that the purely technical discoveries that have been made were not made by chance. The development of oil painting, for instance, depends on nothing more revolutionary than the mixing of dry pigment with oil instead of with yolk of egg or any of the other vehicles commonly used before the fourteenth century. It might seem mysterious that this simple invention had not been made earlier, but the need for it had not yet arrived. It was not an invention made for invention's sake but a development evolved to meet a new need, just as the laws of perspective were not formulated by scientists in pursuit of truth but by artists in search of a means of grappling with the world of phenomena. As long as the artist's main preoccupation was with contour and structure, the media of tempera and fresco were entirely adequate, but once he had begun to be conscious of the surface enclosed by the contour and the play of light across the structure— *inevitably* later developments in the process of *seeing*—those media became unsatisfactory. For the painter's new purposes they ceased to be eloquent. Tempera was as incapable of expressing the shimmering variations of tone on a surface as *thick* oil paint was of expressing the tensions and modulations of line that were the common language of an earlier generation of painters.

Yet the change took place gradually. Giovanni Bellini's first full-scale essay in the new medium was probably the Madonna of St. Job altar-piece, painted in about 1480. Already there is a richness of surface texture and an emphasis on breadth of shadow that were new in his work, and it is significant that he has attempted, in the architectural background, to depict a semi-dome encrusted with gold mosaic—

Giovanni Bellini, Madonna of St. Job

Accademia, Venice

surely the most 'painterly' effect that an artist could tackle. It would not be true to say that tempera would have defeated Bellini's purpose. It is a transitional picture. But it would be true to say that hardly any Venetian picture painted after 1500 could have been painted without

Titian, 'Ariosto Portrait'
National Gallery, London

the oil medium. One has only to look at the sleeve of the so-called Ariosto' portrait by Titian in the National Gallery (1508) to see how the visual preoccupations of the artist have changed. The rippling surface remains in the memory. Its shape is meaningless. Titian's early frescoes in Padua (1511) have an uncomfortable air. Not that Titian

Titian, Christ Crowned with Thorns
Pinakothek, Munich

lacked the skill to manipulate the fresco medium, but that the potentialities of fresco are unrelated to the intentions of Titian. In his hands it
cannot attain the eloquence which it had for Raphael.

The vital—but unanswerable—question is, how far does the medium
suggest a new set of intentions to the artist, or how far can it release
and encourage a set of latent, half-realised intentions? It is certain that
Bellini, discovering to his delight the *ease* with which oil paint would
respond to his growing realisation of surfaces, was encouraged to
concentrate even more whole-heartedly in his next picture on that
aspect of visual experience: but that, having at that stage of his career
(he was fifty when he painted the St. Job altar-piece), formed a set of
technical habits, he found himself unable to push the new medium's
potentialities to their logical conclusion. It was easier for Titian, in

(Anderson photograph)

Leonardo da Vinci, Drawing

Accademia, Venice

84

Rembrandt, Drawing

his early thirties, before technical mastery had hardened into habit, to use oil paint as he used it in Ariosto's sleeve; and, having done so, to continue for the rest of his life to explore the possibilities of the medium until he reached the point where he could concentrate almost entirely on surface-shimmer, as in the 'Christ Crowned with Thorns', in Munich, of 1570. The greatest technical innovators have not, usually, been the original experimenters in a new medium, but the men who followed them and were able to speed up the tempo of the change.

But it is fascinating to note how, once the change has taken place and the artist's vision has been modified by his medium, *any* medium will serve to express it. For example, one might have thought that no medium would be less capable of expressing the play of light on surfaces than pen and ink; and that of all media, sculpture could never avoid expressing it. Yet one has only to compare a pen drawing by Leonardo, however rapid, with one by Rembrandt, or a portrait bust

85

by Donatello with one by Bernini, to see how deliberately the Rembrandt drawing avoids calling attention to the contour and refuses to be explicit, or even graceful, in its line. The emphatic lines used have no linear counterpart in Nature. The scribble of parallel lines over the back of the near disciple (see p. 85) are not contours but an indication of the precise angle as the figure leans suddenly backwards in surprise. The parallel lines on the back of the Virgin in Leonardo's drawing follow and explain the *form* of the figures, and are therefore, in essence, a series of contours like the contour lines on a map. Donatello, though he is employing a medium that deals in surfaces, somehow rivets one's attention on the line of the folds of drapery or the line of the lips, nose and cheekbone. Bernini goes out of his way to break such lines and to defeat the eye's attempt to follow them through, carefully conceals the

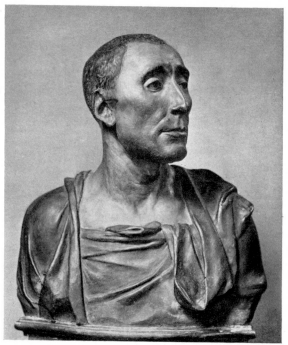

(*Alinari photograph*)

Donatello, Bust of Niccolò da Uzzano

National Museum, Florence

(Alinari photograph)

Bernini, Bust of Francesco I d'Este

Estense Gallery, Modena

contour of the cheek against the broken curls of the wig, and obscures the hard sweep of the metal shoulder-piece against an irresponsible flutter of drapery.

The object of this short chapter is not to describe what effect the medium can have on a painter's vision, but to draw attention to the way in which this two-way traffic of command and request, domination and yielding, operates between the painter's soul and his hand.

Again, as so often before, in analysing the genesis of a work of art, one is brought face to face with this phenomenon of a balance of forces, a set of intersections between factors that seem, at first sight, to conflict with each other, but in the end achieve a balance on which the total effect of the work of art depends.

CHAPTER VI

The 'Mystical Marriage of St. Catherine'

IT WILL CLARIFY MY GENERAL ARGUMENT IF I TAKE A SINGLE painting and submit it to a brief analysis on the lines I have indicated in the previous chapter. Any painting will serve, but in the interest of impartiality it will be advisable to choose one that does not belong to our own time, lest the artist's personal set of loves and hates, preferences and boredoms, should be too unfamiliar and disturbing. And for the same reason, a picture fairly representative of its period and of the place of its origin will be preferable to one that made, even in its own day, too novel, too personal a contribution. Veronese's 'Mystical Marriage of St. Catherine' in Venice (see folded illustration at end of book) fulfils these conditions well enough. It is representative of Veronese, just as Veronese is representative of the Venetian School of the mid-sixteenth century.

Its outer representational skin presents no difficulties. The legend of the Alexandrian saint who, renouncing all earthly ties, was privileged to enter into a mystical alliance with the infant Jesus, was a popular one in the sixteenth century. Any artist commissioned to paint an altarpiece for a church of St. Catherine had his subject set for him. There is therefore no question of Veronese 'choosing' the theme. The subject of the picture has no significance for us as a revelation of Veronese's temperament. The fact that St. Catherine was regarded in his day as "one of the fourteen most helpful saints" throws a sidelight on the development of religious thought, but to enquire into the reasons for St. Catherine's popularity would be to analyse, not our onion, but the field in which it grew. Veronese's representation (as opposed to his interpretation) of the legend is clear. The saint, a Venetian matron dressed in an elaborate and expensive dress of the period, ascends the richly carved steps leading to a throne on which the Virgin is seated.

88

The Child in her lap places the ring on St. Catherine's finger. Three attendants are with her, two of them watch the ceremony while the third looks up with an appropriate gesture to a sky peopled with cherubs, two of whom are descending with a crown. Angels adoring or making music attend the Virgin. Two fluted Corinthian columns complete the architectural setting. The impossibility of distinguishing between an artist's description and his comment or interpretation becomes evident as soon as one attempts to put the picture into words. The elaborate dress, the carved steps, the fluted columns are themselves a comment. An opulence pervades the picture which belies its subject. It almost looks as though Veronese had been at pains to eliminate every hint of the mystical. Certainly no one who was not familiar with the legend would easily guess at the kind of mystery he was depicting. The effect is of a decorously conducted social ceremony. What would have been easy for almost any fifteenth-century painter—a Piero della Francesca or a Sassetta—is impossible for Veronese. The Renaissance, which for two centuries has been pursuing its steady exploration of the material world, has by this time left the mystical world too far behind. The whole meaning of St. Catherine's refusal of an earthly marriage is cancelled out, partly by Veronese's power to represent so adequately the texture of the material world—a power he inherited from and shared with other Venetian painters of his own and the preceding generation—and partly by his particular feeling for material opulence, his incapacity to hint at the deeper implications of this or indeed any other religious theme. Titian, despite his undercurrent of worldliness, seldom failed when he wished to suggest tragedy and mystery. In him and in Tintoretto there is a depth of human understanding that often finds itself in conflict with worldliness, but can always emerge victorious from the conflict whenever the theme demands it. With Veronese, despite his high seriousness, there is no conflict. He is partly a victim of the time-spirit and partly a creator of it. The climax of the High Renaissance, that critical moment when almost everything was possible in art, is past, and Veronese, for no other reason than that he was born fifty years too late, is on the downward slope. That he is content to be so can be seen from the assurance with which he tackles his problem. His confidence in his own world helps to accelerate the descent. This is no picture of a mystical marriage. It is a picture of Venetian citizens taking part in a pageant representing the event. That could not have been said of any Venetian artist before him, not even of Carpaccio. He marks the point at which the spiritual overtones of the Middle Ages finally disappear and leave the field free for the later Baroque attempts to find a substitute for them.

But if Veronese was debarred, through no fault of his own, from painting the deeper aspects of his subject, his contribution to art was not on that account negligible. To dismiss him as 'worldly' without asking what are the positive virtues of worldliness would be like condemning a palace because it was not a cathedral. Incapable of conceiving a cathedral, Veronese is without rival in the construction of palaces.

It is at this point that our enquiry brings us to the second layer, the layer of interpretation. Veronese's comment on his given theme is absurd, but his interpretation of life is as remarkable as it is personal. No one has ever expressed radiant well being, no one has ever painted the ornate seemliness and dignity of human civilisation as he has. Asceticism has been left behind, but decadence has not yet set in. It is a moment of balance—not the earlier balance between body and soul, but the balance between the body and the forces of earthly exuberance or, later still, of intellectual sophistication that are ready to attack it once the soul has lost its ascendancy. The attack has not yet developed; indeed, it would be truer to call it a moment of transition rather than of balance.

Every period has its destined place in the rise-and-fall pattern of civilisation. And every period, because of its place in the pattern, has its own potentialities, a set of values that belongs to it and to no other. In every age an artist emerges to express those values more convincingly than his fellows, and Veronese achieved as complete an expression of the spirit of his generation as any artist has ever done.

Such a statement cannot be substantiated by argument, for it is only by looking at an artist's work and at that of his contemporaries that we know what his generation stood for. But in the paintings of men who are completely in tune with their surroundings, men born neither before nor after their time, one is always aware of a superb confidence. And that confidence—as though he knew that whatever he did, however novel or astonishing it might be, it would never puzzle or embarrass his contemporaries—is the mark of Veronese. Even when the Inquisition took him to task for the excessive materialism of his 'Feast in Levi's House' painted for the Dominicans of SS. Giovanni e Paolo, his answers to the interrogators read like those of a man who knows that he has public opinion on his side. His interrogators might be technically in the right, but they were clinging to an old-fashioned set of standards which neither Veronese nor his patrons could take seriously.

Veronese's worldliness is unique in painting. It is so noble and serious, and yet so friendly and informal. It is radiant with health and normality, and yet dazzling and exotic. The elaborate architectural settings never overweigh the figures, nor do the costly fabrics diminish them. Sanity and splendour combine in equal proportions. His figures are never troubled. No expression on their comely faces contributes much to his meaning, no gesture ever expresses more than a generalised contribution to the action. Giotto, for whom gesture was all-important in establishing the inner meaning of his narrative, or Leonardo, always on the alert to discover the connection between a man's mind and his actions, would have found Veronese a superficial decorator and his St. Catherine an overdressed doll. Yet in spite of, and also because of, his disregard of drama, he is able to establish his unmistakable mood more surely. It is the mood of a man so content with the surface of life that he rarely feels disposed to go behind it. More than that, he is so much in love with it that his paintings become lyrical. They are elaborate odes in praise of seemly living. Even the four angels who make music on the steps on the left are additions to the social amenities of the ceremony. They are as solid as their lutes and the abandoned viol da gamba. The two singers are assiduously reading their score. Their wings are a relic of a past age, and Veronese suppresses them as far as he dare.

Such men have one advantage over profounder artists. Their work has unity and breadth. Nothing seems to them unimportant or irrelevant; therefore everything contributes to the total effect. To a Michelangelo, for whom nothing matters but the majesty of the single individual, the accessories of life are a positive barrier between him and his theme. His Adam and Eve inhabit no desirable garden because he himself is incapable of desiring a garden. But for Veronese the spectacle of Life is an ensemble in which clouds, columns, brocades and

Veronese, Feast in Levi's House

Accademia, Venice

jewels are not mere accessories to his crowds of citizens and angels. They amalgamate with them.

He is, in fact, a stage designer who conceives his scenery and costumes as an integral part of the play. He is not the first to have done so, but he is almost the first to have done nothing else. It is essentially a Venetian characteristic, and the first to practise it on a grand scale was Carpaccio, whose temperament so closely resembled Veronese's. Allowing for the stylistic changes during a half-century of exceptionally rapid development, the parallel between the two men is very close. Colourful but dignified pageantry was the basic theme of both, and occasionally, in moments of greater sensitiveness, both could produce a 'freak' picture that is simpler than usual and strikes a little deeper. Carpaccio's 'Vision of St. Ursula' is such a picture, and so is Veronese's 'Vision of St. Helen'.

Closely related to Veronese's manner of feeling about his world is his way of seeing it. But here he is not quite such a recognisable child of his age. It is not always easy to disentangle the mode of seeing from the things seen, especially in a picture so packed with contemporary documentation as this. The fact that he was more interested than Titian or Tintoretto in the specific appearance of contemporary architecture, ornament and dress led him to be more specific in his painting of them. And that, in its turn, forced him back to a slightly anachronistic way of looking at things in general. In an age when the technique of painting was rapidly becoming broader and more Impressionist, Veronese clung, in many respects, to the harder manner of the first half of the century. The folds of drapery are more explicit. The light is more evenly distributed, the surfaces have less vibration, the patterns are more strongly marked. Veronese's way of *seeing*, on which this is based, is that of the earlier Titian—the Titian of 'Sacred and Profane Love' and the Pesaro altar-piece. He has certainly not reached the point at which Tintoretto had arrived—of massing his shadows in great blocks of darkness and of not caring if his outlines and his local colour were obliterated in the process.

"Has not reached the point" may seem a meaningless phrase if an artist is thought of as having perfect freedom to choose his own way of 'seeing'. But his freedom is by no means perfect. It is bound within very narrow limits. When a painter uses an outmoded idiom, it is because of his innate conservatism: it is never because he has understood but rejected the idiom of his day. Veronese's explicitness of form and his refusal to mass his shadows more boldly are the outward manifestations of an attitude of mind. An artist sees only what he wishes to see, and he wishes to see only what he loves. Veronese loves the richness and the fall of material, and in the area of his picture beneath St. Catherine's extended arm, which Tintoretto would certainly have thought of as being lost in shadow, he cannot bear to abandon his eye's search for the folds of drapery. Tintoretto's habit of letting the shadow cut across the form (note the head of Christ in his Deposition) is so unnatural to Veronese that in only one of the heads in the crowded lower half of the picture—the head that fits in above St. Catherine's bent elbow—does he allow himself to adopt it, and even then he does it half-heartedly.

His planning in depth, too, is out of date. The daring movements

(Anderson photograph)

Tintoretto, Deposition

Accademia, Venice

94

(*Anderson photograph*)

Tintoretto, Presentation of the Virgin
Church of the Madonna dell'orto, Venice

into and out of the picture, that are so characteristic of Tintoretto, are useless to Veronese. Remembering that other progress up a flight of steps in Tintoretto's 'Presentation of the Virgin', in which the fore-shortened arm of a woman in the near foreground positively hurls the spectator into the middle distance where the Virgin stands facing the High-priest at the top of the steps, this side-to-side movement of Veronese's, in which the action takes place 'down stage' and in a plane parallel to the plane of the picture itself, again strikes one as timid. Living at the very moment when movement in depth is becoming one of the artist's major problems, Veronese refuses to concern himself with it.

I have called him a stage designer. So to some extent is every artist, in that he disposes the elements in his picture in the way that will be most effective for the spectator. And, in particular, every Venetian artist in the succession from Jacopo Bellini had been conscious that his stage design must consist of a convincing environment *containing* his actors, rather than an effective grouping of actors to which a backcloth and wings could be added. That had, of course, been the Florentine method, and Jacopo's sketch-books are a vigorous protest against it. But the effect established by Jacopo, perfected by his sons and enlarged by Giorgione and Titian, was still of a stage seen from an auditorium. One is as conscious of the picture-plane, and especially of the lower edge of the frame, as one is conscious, in a theatre, of the footlights, the near edge of the stage.

Tintoretto, by the simple device of imagining himself *on* the stage (and thereby dragging the spectator with him), revolutionised for a whole century the science of picture planning. At once it becomes not only possible but natural to witness a Last Supper or a Crucifixion from the side or a Nativity from below. He compels the spectator to become one of the actors; the footlights disappear, and with their disappearance vanishes one's sense of the picture-plane, that impalpable veil that cuts the spectator off from the world he looks at. One is in the same room as Jesus and His disciples, one is at the foot of the cross, one becomes a shepherd looking up at the Mother and the new-born Babe.

The revolution had little effect on Veronese. Pageantry being his theme, it was essential that he should retain the veil that separates the actors from the audience. The picture's arrangement must be from side to side. Movement must take place across the canvas, not into it.

Nothing could more clearly prove the interpenetration of the layers of the onion than the fact that in describing Veronese's temperament one finds oneself becoming imperceptibly involved in an examination of his system of design. There is no abrupt transition between the artist's attitude to life and his æsthetic. At what point in our analysis can we say that we have now transferred our attention to the æsthetic layer, if it is possible to pass, without a break in the argument, from noting a man's particular kind of worldliness to describing his particular method of picture planning? Yet, though his method of picture-planning is his only way of expressing his attitude to life, it includes much more than the phrase, in its everyday connotations, usually implies. And that 'more' is the purely visual beauty which it is the object of this book to isolate and to see in relation to the other values contained in the work of art. It may be true to say that there is no fixed point at which the transition between the interpretation of life and the creation of beauty takes place, but it is certainly possible to reach a point at which one can be sure that it *has* taken place. Once we find ourselves using the language of mathematics, we can be sure that we are no longer looking at the picture as an interpretation of a man's emotional attitude to the world he lives in. It has begun to take on a formal aspect which cannot be explained by references to the legend of St. Catherine or the spirit of sixteenth-century Venice or the relationship between Veronese and his environment, but which can be hinted at by saying, for example, that Veronese has, in this picture, made extraordinary use of a slowly mounting diagonal that moves in a kind of counterpoint against a set of horizontals and verticals.

That is the kind of phraseology the art critic is sooner or later compelled to use, and as soon as it appears the reader's attention inevitably slackens. The reader is no more than human; he may understand, but he can hardly be expected to enjoy, a description of a mathematical figure; for the description, however accurate, cannot achieve the effect of the figure itself. It cannot appeal direct from the eye to the mind. The words 'diagonal' and 'vertical', however clear their meaning, have none of the immediate emotional effect of a diagonal or a vertical line. The verbal equivalents for such lines would be, perhaps, 'energy' and 'aspiration'. No wonder, then, that critics, as soon as they begin to analyse the mathematical basis of a work of art, and to see the painting as architecture or the architecture as music, tend to become wearisome. To say that a Gothic cathedral is dominated by verticals is true, but it leaves out of account the important fact that a set of vertical rhythms has a special power of thrilling the eye, turning the beholder into a lover. If it were possible to explain the process whereby mathematics engenders love, and the rhythms of a cathedral produce a feeling in the beholder which only the word 'beautiful' will express, art criticism would be easy. The problem here is not the same as that of beauty in Nature. Certainly both depend on a recognition of orderly and law-abiding behaviour, but since the natural laws that produce a pine forest are inevitable, unalterable and universal, the notion of criticism of them does not and cannot arise. But the laws that produced the similar rhythms of the cathedral, being laws based on human *preference*, can only be examined in the light of human preference. If the whole of the thirteenth century in western Europe fell, literally, in love with vertical lines, then we of the twentieth century can only see their work as 'beautiful' in proportion as we can share their love.

It is not difficult for us to do so, for love is both infectious and narrow. By isolating and intensifying his verticals, the Gothic builder could stress them and interrelate them far more effectively than could happen in any pine forest where no such process of isolating or intensifying of a single theme has been at work. We can 'catch' the enthusiasm of the artist in a way that is impossible with Nature, whose forms are not the product of enthusiasm.

But to 'catch' the artist's intention by infection is one thing. To translate it out of his chosen medium into words is another. It can be done to some extent on all the outer levels, but not on the æsthetic level. The effect of a Gothic cathedral can only be expressed in visual terms. The eye alone, without any assistance from knowledge or reason, communicates the visual message to the brain, where it becomes translated into æsthetic emotion as surely and as mysteriously as the white light that falls on a geranium is translated into what we call 'red'. In order to translate that particular emotion into words, one would have to resort to verbal imagery about the lark ascending, the soaring rocket, the upward glance of the saint in ecstasy. Yet just as these concrete images are included in and transcended by the pure mathematics of the cathedral, so does Veronese's series of diagonals include and transcend his narrative of the legend of St. Catherine.

The critic, then, must choose between writing a poem which will be the emotional equivalent of Veronese's pure architecture, and undertaking a cold analysis whose only virtue will be to point out how Veronese's architectural idiom differs from that of other artists.

It is certainly not a revolutionary idiom. Veronese was not an originator, but his power to carry existing inventions a stage further was remarkable. Consider, for example, this device of the diagonal. It is an inevitable result of the decision to abandon the earlier device of symmetry—the chief basis of pictorial composition throughout the preceding century. Symmetry, the placing of the main accent in the centre and building up to it on either side, resulted in the pyramidal composition familiar in formal altar-pieces throughout the fifteenth century. Titian's 'Pesaro Madonna' (painted in the early twenties of the sixteenth) is perhaps the first major protest against the domination of the pyramid, and it must be looked upon as the prototype of Veronese's picture. All the elements are there, the Madonna enthroned high and to the side, the steps leading upwards from left to right, the sequence of figures ascending them, the group filling the vacant corner under the new diagonal, the two columns, the open sky and the cherubs. But Veronese's confidence in an asymmetrical scheme is greater than Titian's. Titian must have felt the need to compensate for his bold removal to one side of the enthroned Virgin and the consequent danger to his picture's stability, by balancing her with the great mass of the Pesaro family banner, by steadying the whole with an emphasis on the horizontal steps and the rectangular throne, and an even stronger emphasis on the farther of the two columns by setting its darkest edge against a radiant cumulus cloud.

Without the 'Pesaro Madonna' Veronese could never have planned his St. Catherine. With it he found courage to go beyond it. The diagonal movement in Titian's picture rises to a climax in the Virgin's head and sinks down again along the arm of St. Francis. There is a similar sinking in Veronese's picture along the playing angel's lute and the singing angel's wing and arm. But now it is subsidiary. The main movement is carried on by two angels *above* the Madonna, and still further by the absurd invention of the drapery wrapped round the columns, and finally vanishes with a tiny triangle of luminous sky at the picture's edge. .

Not content with this main theme, Veronese starts another, rather steeper, diagonal in the left-hand corner, beginning with the viol da gamba and running upwards in a broken but energetic ascent through the four musician-angels.

It would be tedious to work out the picture's scheme in detail. The reader can easily do it for himself, if he is interested. What is important is to note the stage at which Veronese has arrived in the transition from Titian's first daring protest against symmetry to Rubens's complete acceptance of the diagonal in his famous 'Descent from the Cross', in which all trace of symmetry has disappeared and the necessity for steadying horizontals and verticals is no longer felt. Veronese, for example, still feels the need to refer to a centre line sufficiently to arrange his aerial cherubs roughly into a festoon whose centre is also the picture's centre, with the crown-bearing cherubs making a strong diamond-shaped feature in the middle. Below them the upward gaze of the saint's attendant, and above them a particularly emphatic cloud, form a rudimentary centre line—the last vestige of the line which would once have been the backbone of such a composition.

These main constructional lines are, as it were, the picture's skeleton, but the skeleton is not all. Texture or pattern, which means large-scale texture, is another ingredient in the æsthetic sum, and Veronese's texture is an important factor in his final effect. Considered as pattern, the painting has an unusual and enchanting density. Not only are the figures more closely packed than is habitual with his contemporaries, but each figure contains within itself a more consistent pattern. The ripples that dance across its surface are smaller and closer, and they have suaver, gentler rhythms. Nowhere do they become violently agitated, but nowhere are they allowed to disappear. The fluted columns and the carved steps are, on another level, indications of a liking for elaboration in architecture, but on this level they show Veronese's abhorrence of plain surfaces of paint. The columns and the steps in the 'Pesaro Madonna' are smooth, the sky less patterned, the draperies less evenly furrowed with folds. Again the parallel with architecture is inevitable. The 'Pesaro Madonna' has a texture comparable with the West Front of Chartres. 'The Marriage of St. Catherine' is more like Rheims, where an even roughening of the surface with masses of smallish sculpture increases the richness but detracts from the dignity of the façade as a whole. Titian is in all respects a greater artist, but apart from the relative statures of the two men, Veronese's general texture is a later as well as a less noble invention. It was inevitable that he should aim at greater richness, just as it was inevitable that Rheims should be richer and smaller in texture than Chartres. The tide had set in: every artist can contribute to the Zeitgeist, but only at exceptional moments can an artist reverse its direction, and the second half of the sixteenth century was certainly not one of them.

In my exposition of the onion's structure, I had to admit that the core is a mystery beyond the reach of words. There is no need to repeat

(Anderson photograph)

Titian, Pesaro Madonna

Church of the Frari, Venice

(Anderson photograph)

Veronese, The Mystical Marriage
of St. Catherine

Accademia, Venice

(Bulloz photograph)

Rubens, Descent from the Cross

Antwerp Cathedral

(*Donald McLeish*)
Chartres Cathedral, West Front

or elaborate that confession now. It is less possible to throw light on a particular act of creation than to discuss the creative act in the abstract. The spectator and the creator are face to face, and if they cannot make intuitive contact with each other on this level, no third person can help. The only appropriate remark is a reminder to the spectator that in looking at a reproduction, however good, he is not looking at the picture. Ninety per cent. of what goes to make its 'handwriting' is obliterated. The final contact between Veronese and the reader of this book can only be made in the presence of the painting itself.

In our daily experience of life there is no parallel to the phenomenon of interpenetration. In the world of matter it is not possible for more

(Donald McLeish)
Rheims Cathedral, West Front

than one thing to be in the same place at the same time. Even a specially constructed onion with layers fading into each other as well as enclosing each other provides no parallel. Even could it be seen by X-rays, whereby all the layers can be seen simultaneously, the analogy would break down. For in the work of art, though the layers undoubtedly exist and their relative levels lie in the order I have attempted to describe, yet each is an *aspect* of the others and each nourishes and intensifies the others. Remove a single one and the others become impoverished and begin to lose their own significance.

When the 'abstract' artist deliberately removes the outer in order to concentrate on the inner layers, he is presumably content with a smaller onion, but he fails to realise that the result is not only smaller but poorer. The mutually cumulative effect whereby the look of the visible world enriches the artist's sense of harmony, and his sense of harmony quickens his perception of the physical world, is lost as soon as the artist begins to sacrifice any portion of his birthright. The impoverishment is evident enough when, through the unavoidable limitations of the artist's temperament or imagination, one or more of the layers becomes thinner than the rest. Veronese's incapacity for tragedy or ecstasy is a case in point. But when the artist voluntarily and deliberately limits himself still further, he does so at his peril. A boxer who shackles his feet because of a theory that boxing becomes somehow 'purer' if its practice is confined to the arms and fists, actually limits the potentialities of his arm-and-fist work.

It is only when one layer is allowed to develop at the expense of the rest that art becomes mediocre or contemptible. The magazine cover in which feminine seductiveness, or the comic strip in which narrative clarity has absorbed all the artist's creative impulses, are contemptible, not because of their insistence on sex appeal or their concentration on anecdote—Titian and Boucher could rival them in the former, Giotto and Goya in the latter—but because of their lack of enrichment from the inner layers. They are hollow and for the same reason that abstract artists are small. In their case, not the outer but the inner layers are missing.

The number of artists who have developed themselves with equal power at all levels is not large. They are the men who have produced the greatest art, though it would not necessarily be true to say that they were the greatest geniuses. Genius is probably less rare than is generally supposed, but it is not the only factor required for such an achievement. Genius, in order to come to full fruition, must synchronise with the favourable moment in history, and such favourable moments occur only at long intervals. When they do, great artists appear with a frequency that could not be explained if the law of averages alone were operating. That Botticelli, Michelangelo, Leonardo, Raphael, Titian, Giorgione and Giovanni Bellini were all alive and mature in the year 1510, and that they all happened to be of North Italian birth, is no coincidence. Nor is it a coincidence that no European artist of more than mediocre stature was alive in 1680.

This is not the place to discuss the factors that produce favourable moments. Certain artists—Giotto, for example—by virtue of their genius, have occurred in unfavourable moments, and have, none the less, managed to develop on all levels. But in general the great geniuses have depended for development as much on the fructifying properties of their environments as on their own potentialities. Had they been born in another century they would have been lesser men, in the sense that the even balance, the complete interpenetration of the different layers of their work would have been upset. Almost always these men became famous in their own day, for they all possessed that easily understood humanity which Tolstoi wrongly thought of as the test of great art. But only posterity has seen their true greatness; for their creative power does not become apparent until generation after generation has contemplated it and understood it; until it has survived the switchback of taste and proved itself valid by the varied succession of tests to which the centuries submit it.

Raphael's meaning for his contemporaries was very different from his meaning for the mid-nineteenth century: and we, in the twentieth, see him differently again. But the fact that his art was rich enough to satisfy the demands of four centuries so different in their values is the surest proof of his stature. But Raphael was a product of the favourable moment. Never was the soil of civilisation as rich or its climate as benign as it was in Rome between 1500 and 1510. The Venetian soil that nourished Veronese in 1560 was beginning to be impoverished. Perhaps that sufficiently explains the slight lack of balance, the slight thickening, in his case, of the outer at the expense of the inner layers.

CHAPTER VII

The Amalgam

THERE IS NO NEED TO PLEAD FOR VERONESE. 'BEAUTIFUL' IS AN EASY adjective to apply to his St. Catherine picture; for all its qualities —its healthy optimism, the absence in it of anything at all painful or profound or even difficult, its suavity, its luxury and, on the purely æsthetic level, the easy swing of its composition—recommend themselves instantly to the normal eye and the normal mind. And yet when one compares the picture with an actual experience that might conceivably have occurred, how much more satisfying, for all its limitations, is the work of art. A guest, privileged to be present when a Venetian lady of fashion of the 1560s was paying a state visit to her friend, would have received a very different impression. However elaborate the architectural setting, however accomplished the winged musicians, however rich the dresses, the guest would never have summed up the experience as 'beautiful'. And yet the experience would have held far more for him than the picture. He would have heard the voices of the singing angels, the rustle of the brocaded dresses: he would have felt the wind on his cheek: his eye would have been entranced by movement as well as form: he would have heard the conversation that passed between the Virgin and her saintly visitor. The sum total of sensations and perceptions would have been far more complex and far more interesting. Why not, then, more 'beautiful'?

In so far as the answer is "because it comes to us transmuted by Veronese's exceptional temperament", it has already been given in the last chapter But the more fundamental answer, "because it is not a direct experience but a work of art", must now be elaborated a little.

The work of art is isolated, self-contained; it is separated from 'real life' by a frame, and the frame's importance is not only physical but psychological. Not only does it isolate the picture from its surroundings, but it enables one to see the picture in quite a different way from its surroundings. It is not so much that the picture *is* beautiful (whereas the actual event which it describes would have been merely interesting) as that the frame compels us to ask, "Is it beautiful?"—a question one does not normally ask of life. If the actual event of St. Catherine's visit in all its completeness, with the movement, the music, the spoken words, the shifting light and the moving air, could be isolated from the rest of 'life', cut like a slice out of time and placed on a stage, within the framework of a proscenium arch, it would begin to acquire the qualities of a work of art; and as it did so, it would begin, not necessarily to *acquire* beauty, but to compel one to ask, "Is it beautiful?" Unframed, considered as a random fragment of the *continuum* of existence, its beauty never comes into question. It belongs to Nature; it is merely functional. One can only ask, "What led up to it?" and "What were its consequences?" "What was its meaning? Did it form a firm link between what came before it and what came after?" But as soon as it is cut out of time, isolated, framed and placed upon a stage, given a beginning and an end, one's attitude to it changes. It becomes an object for contemplation, and according to its power to please when contemplated, it acquires beauty. If the spectator takes one single step from the auditorium of life on to the stage of art, its beauty is shattered. The frame—the dividing-line between the world of art and the world of life, between the world of contemplation and the world of action—has been violated, and the essence of a frame is that it should be inviolable. Outside the frame is the shifting, growing, dying world of which the spectator himself is an integral part; he may choose to be an impassive spectator, but at any moment he is at liberty to plunge into the action, join in the song, offer his arm to the visitor ascending the steps. However impassive he may choose to be, he is still involved in the life around him. Hamlet's insistence on the experiment of the stage-play is the creative artist's insistence on the isolating frame. As long as his mother and his uncle are involved in the untidy comings and goings of real life, there is no hope of isolating and examining their consciences. But by presenting the King with a work of art, his conscience can be caught. Only the King's call of "Give me some light. Away" can break the frame and end the experiment. Inside the frame is a permanent world created by another man, purged of every trace of transience. The eternal flow of cause and effect, of suffering and joy, has been emptied out of it.

It is this very capacity to isolate itself from the world of action and to appeal only to the contemplative faculty in the spectator that makes its impact on him so intense, and makes him so acutely conscious of its beauty or lack of beauty.

The central characteristic of beauty is that it is always an end in itself and never a means to an end. Its very essence consists in its being useless. Every other value in life is desirable because it leads to some-thing more desirable: beauty alone is intrinsically desirable, and only the contemplative faculty can assess its desirability.

Often enough it becomes so entangled with the life of action that its uselessness is not easy to recognise, but a moment's thought will disentangle it. The taste and texture of food and wine, for example, are so involved with their nutritive value that one is apt to forget that hunger for food is not at all the same as a desire for the taste of food. It is only the delicious sensation, the pleasure of the palate, that can be regarded as æsthetic. The usefulness of food, its purely physiological aspect, has nothing to do with contemplation, and the professional wine taster, in his endeavour to isolate the æsthetic aspect of the wine he tastes, refuses to swallow it, knowing that by doing so he violates the sanctity of the frame, mixes a physiological with an æsthetic pro-cess. For the general purposes of living it is extremely convenient to be able to do so, but whoever is going to specialise in æsthetics must, in the practice of his profession, avoid the mixture.

If the reader doubts this ultimateness or uselessness of beauty, he has only to follow the track of any action involving human motive to discover where it leads. Ask any man why he has acted in such and such a manner, and in the end he will be forced to admit that it was in order to enjoy beauty. Beyond that he cannot go. He works for money. He spends the money on a car. He uses the car—when he is not using it to take him to a place where he can earn more money—to transport himself to a more desirable place. The place is more desirable because it is more beautiful. To every "why?"—"why do you work?"—"why do you want money?"—"why do you want a car, food, clothing, a gas-stove?" he has an answer. But to the question, "Why do you want beauty?" he has no answer. Beauty is utterly useless, because it is a stepping-stone to nothing. It is absolutely desirable, because it satisfies the ultimate appetite.

Even Truth and Goodness, usually bracketed with it by philosophers as absolutes, are more functional. Both are means to desirable ends. Without Truth there would be confusion: without Goodness there would be pain. And both pain and confusion interfere with the life of action: to eliminate them by the pursuit of Truth and Goodness is to use Truth and Goodness as means to a more desirable state of things. But because beauty can never be a means, but only the end to which all means are directed, it must be isolated from all other values. And when man, in his capacity as artist, tries to separate it in his work of art, he is compelled to isolate it within the frame. The frame is no more than a symbol, but it is a necessary symbol. Outside the frame, life must be lived for the sake of living. Inside, it can only be contemplated for the sake of enjoyment.

Once the frame has been established, its contents must submit to a new set of laws. Whether the work of art is music, framed in time, or a stage performance, framed both in space and time, or a painting or statue or building, framed in space alone, the work, by virtue of its frame, has a set of well-defined edges and every element in the work must be related to those edges. The laws that compel the creative artist to give shape to his symphony and composition to his picture, rhythm or rhyme to his poem, pattern to his choreography, are not devices invented to give 'beauty' to his work. They are as inescapable as the laws of Nature. The moment the artist puts brush to canvas they come into operation, not because he has willed them to do so, but because the picture has no meaning—almost no existence—without them. If he puts a single spot of red paint on to a rectangular white canvas, at once the redness of the spot relates itself to the whiteness of the canvas, the position of it and the shape of it relate themselves to the edges of the canvas. The new world, the contemplatable as opposed to the livable world, has come into being inside the boundaries of the canvas and, whether the beholder regards it as beautiful or not, he cannot think of it in any other terms. Its beauty may be negligible; it may even strike him as positively ugly, but it cannot be thought of except in terms of beauty or ugliness. The spectator's attitude to the work of art is bound by the "laws of contemplation", and contemplation deals in no other value but beauty.

None the less, it is unfortunate that the only word available to describe such a specific set of emotions should attach itself to so many different *origins* of emotion. It would be convenient if one could narrow down the meaning of 'beauty', as so many critics have vainly tried to do, to æsthetic experience, and invent a new set of words to describe the non-æsthetic experiences which reinforce and are interwoven with the purely visual central experience.

When, in looking at Veronese's picture, one regards it as an experiment in the use of diagonal rhythms, one is justified in saying "that aspect of the picture contains its ultimate secret. That is the skeleton to which all its other qualities are attached; without that skeleton it could not function as a work of art." But one is certainly not justified in adding "therefore let us limit the meaning of the word 'beauty' to that purely visual, architectural aspect". To say that a man cannot function without a skeleton is very different from saying that the skeleton is the man.

In analysing the picture it was necessary to start with the subject-matter and then to proceed by way of Veronese's mode of *feeling*, his attitude to life, to worldliness, to opulence, to seemliness and so on; to his way of *seeing*, his consciousness of space, shadow-masses, of colour-masses, and finally to his abstract organisation of colour and form within the picture frame. Just as there is no other way of dissecting a body than to start with the outer surface of the skin and work downwards through the muscle to the bone. No other method is possible. The difficulty is to remember that in dealing with the non-æsthetic elements in the picture we are still dealing with elements that are not a part of life, even though they refer the mind back to life. They are still elements that require to be *contemplated*, because they are part of a work of art and not a part of life. The figure of St. Catherine in Veronese's picture can be regarded either as a representation of a fashionable Venetian lady or as an abstract arrangement of form and colour; and certainly, considered as a representation, it is richer in association, nearer to 'life', than it is when considered as abstract design. But in both aspects it is still a thing to be contemplated, though with different parts of the mind.

The whole question of the importance of subject-matter would be easier to handle if a new set of words could be invented to make this distinction. In an earlier chapter I referred to the strange mental shock I received when looking at colour photographs of Nature projected on to a screen in a darkened room. By alternately thinking of them as real landscapes seen through a window and as painted pictures attached to the wall of the room, it was possible to transfer oneself at will from the life of action (i.e. the illusion of being *part* of the landscape) to the life of contemplation. And the realisation that precisely the same image on the screen could be beautiful or unbeautiful according to how one thought of it, gave one a clue to the whole problem. Yet the opposition is not really between beautiful and unbeautiful, which are opposite poles of the same category, but between contemplatable and 'shareable', which belong to different categories. 'Shareable' is not quite the right word, but the right word does not exist. I have already pointed out, in Chapter II, that our attitude to Nature must be one of uncritical acceptance, since we are part of it and its laws are our laws, whereas our attitude to a work of art is one of critical assessment, since the work of art is a comment—one of a million possible comments that can be compared with each other. Nature is a *fact*, the only fact of its kind, and therefore not comparable with any other fact.

It is only when an accident occurs, like that of the coloured transparency, that we can be in any doubt as to which of the two categories is being presented to us, and even then the categories cannot be mixed. We have to decide to live in one or other of the two worlds. But the shock of transition from one to the other is exactly what is needed to show us the difference between life outside the frame—God's creation, and life inside it—man's creation.

The same shock of transition from one mode of living to another must have been experienced by many visitors to Madame Tussaud's who mistook the wax figure of the programme seller in the entrance hall for a living human being. To offer sixpence to a real seller of programmes is a normal part of the life of action; to do the same to a waxwork is to violate the sanctity of the frame, to cross the forbidden barrier between life and art, to attempt to act when one is in the kingdom of contemplation.

The artist who mistrusts the intrusion of subject-matter in his work of art, calling it 'literary' or 'sentimental', on the grounds that it distracts the spectator's attention from the purely æsthetic elements in his work of art, and thereby renders it in some way less 'pure', forgets that the purity he pursues so eagerly has already been automatically ensured by the simple fact that his picture is a work of art. Even Madame Tussaud, exercising the subtlest devices of her craft to break down the frontier between life and art, cannot succeed in doing so, though she may momentarily deceive the eye. The difference between the waxwork and the man is just as great as that between a sitter and his highly stylised cubist portrait; it is a difference in kind. And the artist who refuses to tolerate realism or even representation in his picture, on the grounds that to do so is irrelevant to the business of painting, is making a fruitless sacrifice. He is, in fact, mistaking the skeleton for the human being. The only advantage he gives himself in so doing is that he cannot fall, as so many nineteenth-century artists did, into the error of trying to construct a creature of flesh with no supporting skeleton at all.

Once it has been admitted that 'beauty' is an amalgam of every possible type of human experience built round a central visual scaffolding, but that it can only exist as a stimulus to contemplation and has no connection at all with the life of action, the cry of 'purity' can be silenced. At once art becomes limitless, and each artist takes his place in the hierarchy of genius by virtue of his fullness as a man. His capacity to create in terms of pure æsthetics is in no way belittled by the admission, but it takes its proper place in the final amalgam. As a piece of complex geometry Veronese's St. Catherine is just as firmly constructed and even a little more ingenious than Titian's 'Pesaro Madonna', but as an amalgam of human experience translated into paint, it is less rich and less satisfying. There is no other short way of expressing this difference between the two paintings than by saying that Veronese's is 'less beautiful'.

But just as there is an interdependence between flesh and skeleton, so there is an inevitable interrelationship between the different levels of experience that find their expression in a work of art. The deeper æsthetic levels can exist by themselves, but the upper human ones cannot function effectively without support from below. The amalgam can only become richer in proportion to the fineness and strength of the framework. Veronese's power to give us a sense of sumptuous pageantry is dependent on his strength as a purely formal creative artist. Many of his contemporaries must have had just his feeling about the desirable life, but to find the visual equivalent for the abstract idea contained in the words 'desirable life' requires far more than a gift for colour and draughtsmanship. It requires what is vaguely known as 'imagination'—the power to put technical skill at the disposal of emotional experience—and, by combining the two, to produce the exact visual equivalent of experience; in a word, to find the form that will contain the complete experience. Without that power neither superb technical skill nor profundity of experience is of any avail. With it, the artist's only limitation is the quality of his experience. Veronese, who had the power to an extraordinary degree, is an artist of the second rank only because he is a less complete human being than Titian or Giotto or Rembrandt. The 'ceiling' for genius—in theory limitless because man's capacity for experience is in theory limitless— is imposed upon each artist by the limits of his emotional capacity rather than by the limits of his capacity for *expressing* emotion.

True, there have been artists 'born out of their time' for whom the technical means at their disposal were inadequate for the full expression of their personal vision.

One sees, by the difference between their 'finished' work and their sketches, that the original impulse has *not* succeeded in finding a visual equivalent. Those drawings by Leonardo and Claude, executed in a creative fever, full of the original dæmonic germ of a visual idea, contain all manner of qualities that are absent from the final version— whenever a final version exists. For Leonardo the tradition of Florentine figure-painting, as passed on to him by Verrocchio, acted as a brake rather than a release. His whole artistic life must have been an unconscious struggle with a set of painterly conventions, none of which was capable of expressing his meaning. In consequence he is remembered by thousands of drawings that explore an unknown world, and a mere handful of paintings, each of which is hardly more than a successful challenge to his contemporaries. But, in general, the artist manages, somehow, to grow to his own full stature, to 'do justice to himself', because, in general, the artistic tradition out of which he grows provides him with just the kind of visual vocabulary he needs. The additions he has to make to it in order to express his own personal attitudes are trifling, and though it is of the utmost importance to him to make those additions, the method by which they can be made is clear enough to him. Veronese had much of his own to add to the Venetian flavour of his time, but he had only to look back along the curve of development from Carpaccio onwards to see how that curve could be taken just a little farther without needing to give it any violent change in direction. The form appropriate to contain his experience was already there, and very little alteration was needed to make it the perfect medium for saying what *he* had to say.

I know that there will be readers who will object to my using the phrase "what he had to say" as though one could distinguish between content and form. They will point out that "what he had to say" is his whole picture, regarded on each and every level, including the purely æsthetic level. Technically the reader is right in so objecting, but a distinction must be made somewhere between content and form, just as a distinction must be made between a house and its foundations. Technically there is no dividing-line between the two, but for practical purposes it is impossible to discuss art at all without making distinctions based on common sense.

But the familiar distinction between content and form is no more valid or clear cut than the less familiar distinction between different levels of content. I have already pointed out that subject-matter consists partly of pure description, partly of a comment on the thing described, and partly of an attitude to life in general. Regarded as description, Veronese's picture is no more than a visual account of certain people in certain attitudes in a certain architectural setting. What we make of the picture on that level depends entirely on our own knowledge and experience of life. Only in the light of our own experience of the human countenance do we recognise that the expressions on their faces are noble and serene rather than ecstatic or troubled; only because of our knowledge of costume do we know that they are Venetians of the mid-sixteenth century; only because we have carefully observed the people around us do we know that they are expressing by their attitudes and gestures a certain way of living, a certain tempo—that they are not athletic like Titian's, nor agitated like Tintoretto's, nor languid and withdrawn like Giorgione's; only because we have read the history of St. Catherine do we understand the narrative element in the picture.

But the moment we begin to think of the picture as a comment rather than as a narrative, we become less dependent on our own knowledge and experience of life and more caught up with Veronese himself. Instead of referring the picture back to life as we know it, we begin to accept life as Veronese knew it, or rather to compare our own experience with his and to like or dislike his picture according to whether we find his comment on life sympathetic or the reverse. We begin to understand what it was that he loved, and therefore to enlarge our own loves so as to include his. It is no longer St. Catherine herself who surprisingly takes part in a mystical ceremony with as little awe as though she were paying a formal visit to a friend; it is a creature from another world—Veronese's world. As we look at her, we begin to abandon our own standards and to accept his, and with that acceptance comes the beginning of our conviction that we are in the presence of a thing of beauty.

But only the beginning. The content of the picture goes deeper than this. It is not enough to accept his attitude to this particular event. We must go farther and accept his attitude to every possible event— to those he has not painted as well as to those he has. So that just as, on the first level, we judged the picture by our cumulative knowledge and experience of our own life, on this level we can only judge it by our knowledge and experience of Veronese's art as a whole. In order to understand this particular picture we must know all his pictures, make contact with him at every available point, until the St. Catherine is no longer an isolated statement but a sample of the Veronesesque. In other words, the test of the picture is no longer our own set of standards but Veronese's. The picture becomes more beautiful, not because it is like life as we know it, but because it is unlike. This is an experience which, but for Veronese, would never have occurred, and to which we are bound to become more sensitive the more we have seen of his work.

It is at this point that the art historian, with his wider knowledge of art, scores over the layman. It is quite irrelevant to argue that here on the one hand is a particular work of art; there, on the other, a particular spectator; and that the 'appreciation' of Veronese's intention depends entirely on the spectator's sensitivity to the given picture. As he penetrates downwards from the purely descriptive towards the purely æsthetic levels, his experience of life becomes of less importance to him, but his experience of art becomes more important. He cannot understand a pictorial representation of a human being if he has never seen a human being. And he cannot enjoy the formal arrangement of line and colour without previous experience of other formal arrangements. Just as the layman's eye enables him to recognise the subtlest distinctions between one human being and another in real life, so does the art historian's eye make equally subtle distinctions between works of art. In both cases experience has sharpened sensitivity. One has only to remember how a normal housewife, by virtue of her purely visual experience, can judge the exact texture and shade of colour that signify that the joint is properly cooked, the toast done to a turn; or how one can oneself deduce the precise mood of a friend by noting his 'expression' which, after all, consists of the minutest departures from the normal in the set of a mouth, the depth of a wrinkle or the angle of an eyebrow. Max Friedländer describes how an artist at a conference on the design of a new issue of bank-notes suggested omitting the rather commonplace portrait heads introduced into them, but was told that the average bank clerk found the expression on the faces a surer test of forgery than the minutest examination of the ornamental portions of the design. But the housewife's experience of cooking or the normal man's of facial expression is not different in kind from the student's experience of works of art. Experience is the faculty that enables us to interpret the present in the light of our memory of the past. The better stocked our memory, the more subtle our interpretation.

It follows that 'association' plays its part in our sense of beauty, not only on the outer levels of a work of art, but on every level. What has already been said about associational beauty in Nature still applies. The green field patterned with yellow and white spots is more beautiful if the spots are buttercups and daisies than if they are empty cigarette packets and torn-up newspaper. But it is only in the light of our pleasant memories of flowers and our painful memories of litter that the meadow becomes more or less beautiful. Regarded as description, Veronese's St. Catherine picture is more beautiful if it reminds us (i.e. if we can correlate it with our own private recollections) of pleasant or memorable experiences. And since, for most of us, our experience of life is far richer than our experience of art, the outer levels of a painting are richer in associational values than the inner.

But it is not difficult to imagine an assiduous student whose experience of art is as rich as his knowledge of life. To him the handwriting of Veronese's picture, the rhythms, colour-harmonies, tricks of composition, have as many associated values as the subject-matter itself. Indeed, if we define association as the appeal to the spectator's experience, there is no aspect of a work of art that does not make its appeal by association—and by association alone. What makes an artist 'great', and what makes his work 'beautiful', is his power to strike this responsive chord of memory in the beholder—to make himself, in fact, 'understood'. That, of course, is the central theme of Tolstoi's theory of art, but whereas Tolstoi, in assessing the relative 'greatness' of works of art, chose the understanding of the average man as his test, it is manifestly the exceptional man, the man with the fullest store of experience, who must be the judge. And the deeper the level the more the exceptional man becomes the only competent judge.

Almost every human being's experience fits him to respond to the 'sentiment' of a picture—to its dramatic or narrative or psychological message. Leonardo's 'Last Supper' can grip the imagination of mankind for no other reason than that it is a thoroughly adequate presentation of the dramatic implications of the moment depicted. But equally so are a host of mediocre paintings, especially those of the mid-nineteenth century which specialised in sentiment. The average man, with his massive everyday experience of sentiment and his meagre experience of anything else, is puzzled to know why Leonardo's 'Last Supper' is supposed by experts to be so much greater than Leighton's 'Last Watch of Hero' or Watts's 'Hope'. And critics have attempted to show that Leonardo's sentiment was in some way 'truer' or 'more genuine' than Leighton's. They are wrong. Where Leonardo scores is not as a narrator or even as a psychologist, but as an explorer of realms of experience into which the average man cannot follow him. Although Leonardo's picture is now a hardly decipherable wreck and his original subtleties of facial expression have been largely effaced by time and the clumsiness of later hands, the picture is still valid as drama. Yet how easy it would be to destroy that drama by a few malicious touches of the brush—to turn, by a few minor alterations in the line of a mouth or the angle of a brow, reverence into mockery, tragedy into farce. Only a few square inches in that great area would need to be altered. The picture would remain. The deeper realms of experience explored by Leonardo would be unaffected. None the less, the contradiction between them and the more obvious narrative elements would be intolerable. The amalgam would be shattered and even the purist who professed to despise the easy appeal to sentiment could not stomach the result.

Cézanne, for whom the dramatic or sentimental had so little appeal, can never be a popular artist though he is acknowledged to be a great one. Poussin, who paid careful but half-hearted lip-service to this outer level, will never persuade the average man that he was a 'human' painter. For the average man is uncannily alert to the difference between lip-service and sincerity. There have been many artists of this kind, men who, like Velazquez, were temperamentally incapable of interesting themselves in the world of sentiment, or who, like Degas, cynically rejected it. To the average man such artists are uninteresting, because they refuse to meet him on his own familiar ground and insist on his following them into regions of which he has no experience.

It is those unfamiliar regions that the average man has in mind when he says, "I know nothing about art"; and it is to the familiar regions of his own experience that he refers when he adds, "But I know what I like". If he were to probe a little deeper he would proceed to say, "I like those works of art which confirm my own experience of life but present it to me in an intensified form": and if he were willing to accept the logical corollary to this statement, he would have to admit that by enlarging his experience he would also enlarge his power to like works of art which have hitherto been unattractive because incomprehensible to him. In order to do so he would certainly have to 'know' more about art, but not in the sense in which he uses the phrase. He assumes that art is a mystery that can only be properly understood by the specialist, and that such specialisation has nothing to do with the common-sense judgments of the layman.

But what does, in fact, happen when the layman begins to 'know about art' is in no way different in kind from what happens when he 'likes' a work of art. To like is merely to share. To like a picture called the 'Last Watch of Hero' is to share the emotion and to understand the intention of the artist who painted it. Obviously, unless the spectator's experience is identical with the artist's, it is impossible for him to understand the *full* intention of the artist. But instinctively the spectator guesses just how much of the artist's intention has escaped him. He is disturbed and annoyed by the sense that he is in the presence of something beyond his range; and he rationalises his annoyance by calling this something 'art' and dismissing it as being outside his province as a layman. Comparing 'The Last Watch of Hero' with 'The Last Supper', he recognises in both a human drama that he has no difficulty in understanding, but with Leonardo he is less happy than he is with Lord Leighton, for he knows that behind and bound up with the subject-matter of Leonardo's picture there is a great deal that eludes him, but which apparently does not elude the specialist. He can only reconcile himself to such a state of affairs by asserting that what he misses is unimportant because it has something to do with 'art' and nothing to do with 'life'. If the layman were to be quite honest he would have to remodel his favourite phrase. "I know enough about life to like the superficial levels of art, but not enough to like its deeper levels." "I know what I like" is thus translated into "I like what I know". And if he were to be even more honest he would add, "But I know so little".

It should be the critic's major occupation to explain to the layman just what kind of 'knowledge' he needs in order to see in Leonardo's picture something more than a clever representation of a critical moment in the life of Christ; or in Veronese's picture something more than an elegant failure to tell the St. Catherine story or even than a magnificently successful act of homage to Venetian femininity. Yet this very tract of experience, this "something more" which lies between the strongly marked limits of pure description on the one hand and pure geometry on the other, is the most difficult tract for the critic to cover. It is essentially the painter's own private ground. The descriptive elements in his picture join up with the frontiers of literature and can easily find their equivalent in prose; the geometrical elements are definite enough for their main outlines (though not their emotional effect) to be translated into words. But between these two strong supports, joining them together and thereby giving them a functional purpose, is stretched a tenuous suspension bridge of the artist's own; and the creative mood—the excitements, the indifferences, the intuitive leaps, the equally intuitive gropings—responsible for this part of the picture is precisely the mood that tends to evaporate when the critic begins to analyse, and in doing so, deliberately adopts an intellectual, rational frame of mind in which intuition can find no place. The critical attitude, in fact, must be abandoned. Words, if they are to be of any service at all, can no longer *explain* the artist's intentions; they can only hope to find an equivalent for them.

In some ways it is a relief for the critic to lay aside his analytical spectacles and plunge into the same deep waters as the artist himself. He need no longer trouble to search for and offer up grains of truth to the reader. He can now build his own edifice of words in just the same spirit as the artist's edifice of paint, relying on his own intuitive excitements and boredoms, but praying that his intuition will be sturdy enough to save him from mere gush and sentiment.

Every great painting has this quality, that after seeing it some corner of life will never be quite the same again. Some patch of one's potential experience has been vitalised and sharpened, as though it had been not

Carpaccio, St. George Baptises the Princess
Church of S. Giorgio, Venice

Giorgione, The Tempest
Accademia, Venice

merely temporarily illuminated but permanently sensitised. It begins
to have a reality of its own just as distinct from the reality that existed
before, as the sound of a poem is distinct from its sense. The particular
genius of an artist can often be defined by answering the questions,
"What patch has he illuminated for me?" "What things will never be
quite the same again now that I have seen his work?"

But the illumination is cumulative. Each individual artist, adding
his own spotlight to the radiance that emanates from his 'school',
increases the general diffusion. And the more the spectator "knows
about art", the more radiant it becomes. The big patch of light shed
by the Venetian school is intensified in localised areas by individual
painters, each of whom benefits from the radiance of the whole.

There is no need to describe the character of Venetian painting in
detail. Every interested reader knows how it developed out of the

humanism that had been spreading from Florence all through the earlier part of the fifteenth century and had pervaded the cities of northern Italy in varying degrees; how Venice found herself temperamentally incapable of absorbing the intellectual, mathematical and philosophical aspects of humanism that characterise Florentine art, but gradually developed a new mood of sensuousness in which music, languor and the day-dream provide one element and pageantry the other. The first had been elaborated and established for all time by Giorgione, the second by Carpaccio. Without one or other of these two basic moods to stimulate and invigorate it, Venetian art could achieve nothing more than the decorative fancifulness that we associate with Crivelli.

Titian, once he had outgrown the Giorgionesque day-dream, developed an energetic, athletic variant of it: Tintoretto, a new and disturbing turbulence. But despite the extraordinary personal genius of these two artists, the areas they illuminate fall roughly within the general Venetian area. Music, pageantry and the day-dream are still implicit in their work. The intellectual discipline, the clarity, the philosophy of Florence never enter into it.

Veronese, the greatest of the Venetian masters of pageantry, belongs to the more decorative, the less profound branch of the school. There is little enough of the Giorgionesque in his temperament. But he would not have been a Venetian—or rather, Venice would never have attracted him from his native Verona—had he not understood the spirit of the *poesia*, which pictorial art had never conceived before and which it has seldom achieved since. No truly Venetian painter has lacked that understanding. It is precisely this command of sensuous overtones that gives one the sense of entering into a dream as one turns, in the National Gallery, from Mantegna's 'Agony in the Garden' to Giovanni Bellini's version of the same theme. Without it, Bellini could never have painted those disturbing little allegories in the Accademia. Carpaccio could never have imagined the quietude of the 'Vision of St. Ursula', which makes so strange a prelude to the picturesque bustle of the story that follows it. Still less could he have envisaged the torrid stillness of the 'Meditation on the Passion' in the Metropolitan Museum, New York. Titian would never have passed through the phase that produced, ten years after Giorgione's death, the opulent languor of

Crivelli, Virgin and Child Enthroned

National Gallery, London

Giovanni Bellini, Agony in the Garden
National Gallery, London

'Sacred and Profane Love'. Tintoretto could never have accomplished
the 'Bacchus and Ariadne' in the Ducal Palace. Without it and its
three companions one would never have known how completely
Tintoretto was capable of detaching himself from the world of action.

Had this handful of pictures been lost, the corpus of Venetian
painting would certainly not have been robbed of its greatest pictures
(though the 'Sacred and Profane Love' would be a heavy loss), but
some of the most magical interpretations of human emotion would be
unknown to us except through the rare works of Giorgione. Giorgione
would be as isolated a figure as el Greco: a freak without ancestry or
progeny rather than an inspiration.

No great Venetian failed, at some time in his career, to respond to
this mysterious call of the Giorgionesque. Those Venetians in whom
there is no trace of it are those whom we could easily spare—the
Crivellis and their kind. Even the most negligible of the rest are saved
from oblivion because they have it.

What gives Veronese his firm hold over our affections is precisely this quality. In addition to the sonorous swing of his rhetoric, the pomp of his piled-up balconies shining in the blond light of a Venetian noon, despite the athletic grace of his individual figures and the magnificent assurance with which he masses them together, there is always a hint of the Giorgionesque day-dream that enables him to detach himself from the grand company of decorators and pageant-mongers to which he seems to belong by right, and to join the smaller, rarer company of dreamers. Inevitably in this rarer company he takes a lower place. That is one of the paradoxes of his art. Had he been no more than a pageant-monger, he would have been in the same company as Rubens, and second only to him in rank because second to him in sheer energy and fecundity. But since, by virtue of his Venetian poesy, he is greater than Rubens in kind, he is condemned to hold a less exalted position in the higher category.

Much has been written about the Giorgionesque. It is the exact

Mantegna, Agony in the Garden

National Gallery, London

125

opposite of the Rubensesque. Just as it was part of the heritage of every Venetian, so it was completely outside the comprehension of every Fleming. Pater understood it well enough to make every reader of his famous essay realise, once and for all, its curious nostalgic power. But having achieved this consciousness of its full flavour in Giorgione himself and in his followers and disciples, we now begin to be conscious of the subtle dilutions of it in artists who are not temperamentally dreamers, but who caught it unconsciously, merely by breathing the adjacent air.

These elusive overtones are inevitably missed, unless one can induce in oneself a receptive mood quite incompatible with the analytical mood. The attempt made in the previous chapter to analyse the particular achievement of a particular painting was foredoomed to miss them: the frame of mind in which such an analysis is made is incapable of catching flavours of that kind. The only course open to one is to rewrite the chapter in a different frame of mind—the careless, disorderly frame of mind of one who allows himself to drift, instead of deliberately attempting to follow a reasoned path. But such disorderliness can only have fruitful results to a mind already familiar with the generic flavour of the school or schools of painting in question.

Psychologists find their quickest approach to the less accessible levels of memory and experience through the method of 'free association'. "Don't *think* about this: don't isolate it: don't, above all, attempt to explain it. Merely allow it to sink, by its own weight, into your consciousness—and then say whatever comes into your head. That— the unbidden crowd of associations, of released memories—must be the real object of your examination. Explain that, and the original mystery will automatically explain itself." Only by constant practice of the method does it become possible to lay bare the full implications of the particular problem under consideration. Only by making the patient completely *un*-analytical does psychoanalysis become possible.

Exactly the same process must take place if one hopes to 'tune in' to an artist. But the process is only possible if a mass of associations— experiences already piled up by contact with other works of art—is ready to hand. 'Free association' depends, as the phrase implies, on an ample fund of existing experience: the ampler the fund, the more rewarding will the process become. And, oddly enough, it will usually

(By courtesy of Louis Carré Gallery, Paris)

Picasso, Portrait, October 12, 1941

be experiences of art that will arrive most easily, for they come to us purged of irrelevances, and are therefore both sharper and more intense than our memories of everyday life. It is true that certain powerfully original works of art are *not* illuminated by our experience of art. The art of the past has not prepared us for them. The associations do not arrive, because they do not exist. In such cases we can only fall back on our experience of life itself, and if our experience is insufficiently deep or comprehensive, we are at a loss. The failure, not only of laymen but of artists, to see what certain modern painters are driving at is mainly due to this. The original creative artist has taken too little from other artists and too much from life. The usual complaint that their pictures are 'unlike life' is quite untrue. They are, on the contrary, too 'like', but the particular fragment of experience they express is one that has hitherto escaped the spectator. There are, for example, certain paintings by Picasso, whose fierce, spiky rhythms are, I could swear, derived from the fierce spikiness of a thistle leaf. No one, before Picasso, had ever experienced a thistle leaf with such frantic intensity. The first sight of such a painting is bound to be irritating and painful, because it corresponds to no known sensation, and seems, therefore, to be meaningless. But gradually light begins to spread from the picture. The feeling, already referred to, that some aspect of the world will never be quite the same again begins to grow. Picasso has enlarged our sense of life. It may not be possible to explain him in the light of Poussin or Cézanne, but it *is* possible to explain him in the light of thistles.

Veronese was never quite such an originator of new experiences as Picasso. It *is* possible to explain a good deal of him in the light of Venetian art in general and of Carpaccio and Titian in particular. That breaks down our natural resistance to whatever in his painting is new. Three-quarters of Veronese was *not* new, and therefore the remaining quarter—the quarter that makes him so precious to us—is easier to accept. He is a bigger, a more universal artist than Picasso, but his love of the aspects of life that he could make his own was not nearly so intense. His discoveries, which were many and important, were never announced with such uncompromising directness.

Looking at Veronese's picture and allowing it casually to unlock the doors of association, phrases like "the noble life; the desirable life; the pleasures of the senses; linger; taste; listen; enjoy" float unbidden into one's mind. And with them vague memories of the 'Dame à la Licorne' tapestries woven in France a century earlier for a very different kind of patron and an even more different kind of society. Between the two works there can be no connection, cultural or artistic. Veronese breathes the spirit of a proud and sophisticated city; the French tapestry comes from the heart of the feudal countryside. Veronese has the Classic suavity; the Frenchman is angular and crisp and Gothic. Veronese's colour is cool and blond, the tapestry hot and rich. And yet the association persists. The two melodies, so different in shape, so unrelated in harmony, evoke the same mood. It is the mood in which the life of action is arrested, but the life of sensation and contemplation

(Photograph, Victoria & Albert Museum, Crown copyright reserved)
The Lady with the Unicorn
French Tapestry, Cluny Museum

flows exquisitely and gently on. In the French tapestry the lady tastes the fruit, listens to the melody, enjoys the sensations of smell, touch and sight, and finally stands motionless at the opening of her pavilion of sky-blue dotted with little yellow flames, with the inscription '*A mon seul desir*' over her head. She exists only in a dream world to which heraldry, the bestiary, the botanist have all contributed, and which has been given cohesion by the lover and the hedonist. It is a world equally freed from the bonds of action, pain and doubt.

Veronese inhabits—and therefore creates—precisely the same world. In the last chapter I compared him with Carpaccio. But Carpaccio's world—composed of the same ingredients, heraldry, colour, elegance and pageantry—is certainly not freed from the bonds of action. Carpaccio was no hedonist.

Hedonism is not an attractive word to the Englishman. In its un-disguised form—as presented, for instance, by Huysmans in 'A Rebours'—he finds it unpalatable and he labels it decadent. Pater, with his ninety-ish insistence on the "hard gemlike flame", made even Giorgione sound a little unhealthy. But Veronese has none of the taint of decadence; the Englishman understands him because he is a material-ist. Veronese does not *brood* over perfumes and jewels and the dying cadences of the viol da gamba. He *uses* them. He tempers the sensation-hunt of the æsthete with the gross pride of the *nouveau riche*. To the exquisiteness of Huysmans' hero, des Esseintes, he adds just enough of the vulgarity of Sir Gorgius Midas to save him from the frown of the moralist; though that very strain of vulgarity, which for us takes the edge off his preciousness, got him, as we have seen, into trouble with the inquisitors of his own day.

The 'Lady with the Unicorn' escapes from the charge of hedonism by another route. What saves her is not materialism but innocence. Eve, enjoying the good things in the Garden of Eden before the fall, could not have been less open to the charge of decadence. But innocence was impossible in mid-sixteenth-century Venice. The mood of the French tapestries is the mood of spring: of the tightly folded bursting bud and the fresh gamut of sharp, urgent colour. The mood of Veronese is that of early autumn: the full-blown flower and the rich complexity of ripeness.

In the summer of 1947 I saw the picture again. The Church of St. Catherine was an empty shell, with locked doors: the picture had been removed and was to be seen (in a brilliant light, but not the light for which Veronese intended it) in the Accademia. It sur-prised me a little, because the pale cobalt of the sky immediately over the heads of the main group was more intense than I had remem-bered, or than I have ever seen in a picture by Veronese. But it was certainly Veronese's intention to make it so. No later hand has re-painted it. In fact, the painting is in fairly good condition, and the only considerable area of repainting is the Virgin's peacock-green dress below the knee.

The colour of the whole is so marvellously organised that it must be described. For on its colour its mood depends. And though that is true of the bulk of Venetian painting after Carpaccio and Giovanni

Bellini, it is truer of Veronese than of any other Venetian. Other Venetian painters have been equally gifted colourists. It is true of most Venetians and of hardly any Florentines that form and colour seem to have been conceived in the painter's mind as a single entity—as colour-form, not as coloured form. But though a half-tone reproduction of Carpaccio or Bellini always suggests that the colour is somehow resplendent, one cannot always guess in what way resplendent; whereas a half-tone reproduction of a Veronese implies the *kind* of colour harmonies he used. It gives an impression that the whole was painted with the coloured juices of fruits with silver shining through them. One builds up, from the colourless reproduction, an *expectation* of colour which is often exceeded by the original painting but seldom contradicted. In this instance only the patch of pale-cobalt sky contradicted my own expectations.

The rest of the picture is a miracle of colour orchestration, in which the climax is the Virgin herself. Over her rose-coloured dress and peacock-green mantle is thrown a semi-transparent veil of pale grey-green—the colour of the under-surface of olive leaves. These are the colours which are echoed and repeated throughout; they prepare for the climax, but never compete with it. Orchestration is the only word for Veronese's system. Rose and blue-green answer each other like wood-wind and strings, with subtle variations of pitch and intensity within each group. The folds of stuff that embrace the pearl-grey columns are of dull rose. The dress of the angel in the left-hand lower corner, in colder grey brocaded with gold, is lined with pale strawberry, and her narrow girdle is of amethyst. Her companion's cloak is of dark coral. The higher of the two lute players wears a robe of strawberry with sleeves of flashing white. On the right of the picture, among the Saint's attendants, these warm accents diminish, but a glow of amethyst in the figure on the right carries the same note across to the edge of the canvas, while a connecting-link is provided by St. Catherine's under-sleeves, which are dull coral edged with white lace.

The colder colours—the stringed instruments in the orchestral scheme—have a wider range, but they are distributed with equal skill. Their climax of depth is in the Virgin's mantle, but their climax of brightness is in the brocade worn by St. Catherine. This brilliantly patterned dress—it must have been a studio property, for the two kneeling girls in the National Gallery's 'Darius and Alexander' wear dresses of the same pattern—is as vivid and as crisp as Veronese dared to make it without upsetting the picture's balance. It is in two depths of blue—cobalt and ultramarine—on a ground of palest grey. It was probably in order to give support to this coruscation of blue and almost-white that Veronese allowed himself to insert the unusually vivid patch of sky; and deeper blues are carried into the upper half of the picture in the cherubs' wings.

Veronese's pictures are almost always irradiated with silver and shot with gold, but never more skilfully than here. Silver-grey shimmers down the fluted columns, along the carved steps, among the folds of St. Catherine's dress, in the robe of the nearest seated angel. A cold silver light shines through the clouds above. Threads of gold shine elusively among the greys, and the hair of all but the Virgin and two of the Saint's companions is gold—the gold of apricots mingled with the gold of lemons.

Now even if Veronese had been a pure sensualist, with no other intention than to catch the eye in an orchestral web of colour, the picture would still be adorable, for the associations it arouses are adorable. It cannot be described, except in terms of flowers, fruits, precious metals and precious stones. Roses, olive leaves, strawberries and apricots, silver, coral and amethyst, are the only available words. But an orchestral web is not enough, whether it be made of sounds or words or colours. Art depends less on the ingredients than on the amalgam. And in this particular department of the larger amalgam which this chapter attempts to describe, Veronese is un-rivalled. That is why the half-tone reproduction builds up an expectation of colour. The mood engendered by those gracious, unemphatic gestures, the combination of aristocracy and seemliness, is exactly the same mood, though on a different plane, as the luxuriance of flowers and fruits, the glint of metal and precious stone. The two reinforce each other and fuse into a single integrated whole. It is a process not of addition but of multiplication—not of colour plus form, but of colour wedded to form.

Admittedly it is neither profound nor disturbing. Neither aristocratic seemliness nor fruits and precious stones are capable of stirring one's deeper emotions. But precisely for that reason the word 'beautiful' is easily applicable to it. Not that the profundities of the later Titian or the later Rembrandt, or the uneasy ecstasies of el Greco or the outspoken indignations of Goya, are in any serious sense less beautiful. But there is less in Veronese to trouble the mind: there are no glimpses in him of the terrifying unknown, or even of the unwelcome. Ever since, with the advent of the Renaissance, man became self-conscious about beauty and attempted to differentiate between the varieties of its impact, there has been an agreed subdivision of it into suave and sublime. With the High Renaissance the distinction was sharpened. Raphael and Michelangelo were the protagonists of grace on the one hand and sublimity on the other. Both temperaments carried with them their own dangers. The suave ran the risk of cloying through over-sweetness; the sublime was apt to founder on the rocks of melodrama. But what is it that makes one instinctively apply the word 'beautiful' to the gentler and more serene aspects, both of art and of Nature, and hesitate to apply it to their more violent and disturbing manifestations? I think it is a realisation that moods of violence and unease can find a completely satisfactory expression in terms of form, but never quite in terms of colour, and the perfect amalgam can therefore never be attained.

It is not by accident that Michelangelo's colour, though pleasant enough in itself, adds very little to his total effect. And it is not surprising that the later works of Titian are less colourful than the earlier. Again the analogy with orchestration seems appropriate. Titian's 'Entombment' of 1525 in the Louvre is orchestrated in the Veronesean sense; the later, more tragic, version of 1559 in Madrid is no longer delectable. It is far grimmer and more thunderous. His final statement as a painter—the great 'Pietà' he painted as a memorial to himself—is almost colourless. Beethoven, too, in his last years, abandoned the delights of orchestration and made his final statements in the form of string quartettes.

Colour, as already noted, is a sensation—a bombardment of the eye, not a perception by the eye. The appreciation of colour is passive; that of form, active. Consequently, despite the intensity of the æsthetic pleasure or displeasure aroused by it, it can never appeal to the intelligence. And the more deeply the artist penetrates, the less appropriate for his purpose is the kind of colour I have called 'delectable': the more he tends towards the sombre harmonies of the late Titian or Rembrandt.

Now if 'beautiful' has a meaning as distinct from 'exciting', 'moving,' 'impressive', or any of the adjectives one normally uses to describe works of 'sublime' art, it is surely this—that it describes the perfect balance between sensation and perception, between the sensuous and the intellectual. And it is precisely because in the 'sublime' the balance is upset that it differs from the 'beautiful'. Colour can only produce its maximum of sensuous delight at the cost of the intellect. It is impossible to imagine the two otherwise than related to each other, in the sense that the two ends of a seesaw are related. And it is equally impossible to imagine them failing to amalgamate with each other, still less contradicting each other. A drawing by Michelangelo or Rembrandt coloured by Fra Angelico or Matisse would be unthinkable. We may regret that Michelangelo's colour is not more inventive or Rembrandt's more gay, but they could not be otherwise, and no so-called 'great colourist' could help them out with advice or collaboration. 'Beauty' in its strictest sense is only attainable when the fusion between colour and form is perfect, when both issue, at one birth, from the same creative imagination, and when both have an equal impact on our senses.

But both 'amalgam' and 'fusion' are misleading words, for they suggest a set of separate ingredients baked in a kind of artistic crucible over a fire lit by the creative spark. The image is false. It would be equally misleading to describe a human body as a fusion of skin, muscle, nerves, arteries and bones. Any text-book on human anatomy is bound to subdivide the body into its elements, but only for the purpose of convenience in description. Like the human body, the work of art is an organic whole. Art criticism is compelled to describe it piecemeal, but it was not conceived piecemeal. At every stage in its progress from the initial image in the mind's eye of the artist to the final brushstroke, it was an integrated creation, complex and many-sided, like a cut diamond, but single and unified in its texture.

CHAPTER VIII

Taste

PERHAPS THE HISTORY OF TASTE WILL NEVER BE WRITTEN. TO collect the necessary data would require, not only superhuman devotion, but an awareness of the influences that mould civilisation, which no single human being could possess. Moreover, the history of taste is the history of vanished loves and prejudices; and whoever undertakes it will be at a disadvantage in that he will himself be at the mercy of his own active loves and prejudices. Impartiality is an ideal which no historian can achieve, for it is only by having a *parti pris* that he can distinguish between significant and irrelevant events. An impartial history, however free from inaccuracies, would be rather like a map with no indication of the points of the compass. But when the historian is dealing not with events but with that complex of human preferences and disgusts which, added together, produce what is known as 'taste', he must be on his guard against his own taste. He cannot discard it, but he must be aware of it. His picture will certainly be distorted, but if he knows that he is distorting, he will at least be under no illusion that his work can have the finality of an objective record.

The *mechanism* of taste, however (as opposed to its history), can be examined without a *parti pris*. It is, of course, closely related to the creative mechanism of the artist already described in Chapter III. The artist's personal loves and prejudices play a major part in its formation; but art is not the only formative influence in shaping the group-consciousness which in its creative aspect is called 'style' and in its passive aspect 'taste'.

It is a mechanism that could be roughly compared to a sieve whose mesh has the power to sort and reject *qualities* instead of *sizes*. What passes through it at a given moment of time is the raw material that the critic or historian must work on. Without this preliminary passage through the sieve, the material at his disposal would lack homogeneity: it would be unintelligible and therefore undescribable. But if we turn our attention from the material that has passed the censorship of the sieve to the construction of the sieve itself, the art historian is no longer the only man to help us. To discover what makes the mesh and what forces continually change it, involves far more than a study of art. There is no branch of human knowledge from philosophy to social history that cannot shed light on one or other of the factors that determine the taste of a man, a geographical area, a stratum of society or a decade.

Almost every human thought or action contributes its scrap of evidence. And even negative evidence is significant. What a beam of light, for example, is shed by travellers' diaries on the taste of their time, by their failure to understand or even notice what strikes us today as remarkable. The gentlemen who undertook the Grand Tour in the mid-eighteenth century with their eyes adjusted to the beauties of Classic architecture, and to whom a Gothic cathedral was not so much offensive as invisible, are among our best witnesses in an enquiry into the nature of taste. They provide an example of a double sifting. The Classic mesh is placed vertically below the Gothic, and whatever manages to pass through both gives us the common denominator of both.

"Every epoch," says Max Friedländer, "acquires different eyes." He is speaking of the difference between an original and a forgery in painting. He continues, "Donatello in 1930 looks different from what he did in 1870. That which is worthy of imitation appears different to each generation. Hence, whoever in 1870 produced works by Donatello will find his performance no longer passing muster with the experts in 1930. We laugh at the mistakes of our fathers and our descendants will laugh at us."

But forgery is only an extreme case of a process that pervades the whole of life. The attempts of one period to see through the eyes of another are always illuminating and often laughable, but often they are only detectable to the eyes of a third period. The costume and behaviour of a mid-Victorian actress who undertook to present an Elizabethan heroine are, to twentieth-century eyes, symptoms of ludicrous failure on the part of the nineteenth century to understand

Strawberry Hill

Fonthill, from an engraving

137

(*Crown copyright reserved*)
Modigliani, Carving
Victoria & Albert Museum, London

the sixteenth. But our own failure, though different in direction, is certainly the same in kind, and we may be sure that it will be just as ludicrous in the eyes of the twenty-first century.

So different, indeed, is the direction when one period, out of sheer enthusiasm and with no intention of disguising itself, borrows the outward forms of another, that we no longer laugh: we even admire. The Gothic revival which, in the course of its long development from Strawberry Hill in the eighteenth century to Liverpool Cathedral in the twentieth, produced so many different reinterpretations of mediæval forms, has now acquired the respectability and even the merit of an original, creative movement, and the fact that we can at last see it as such is a proof that the movement is virtually finished. We can at last see it in its true relation to its mediæval ancestor, just as we can see Botticelli's Venus in relation to the Venus de Medici, herself a descendant of a Venus by Praxiteles. We know why she is slimmer, more agile, more wistful. We know why her shoulders slope more steeply, and why the axis of her body is so much more lithe and *mouvementé* than that of her Græco-Roman prototype. We know that Botticelli's creative imagination was the product of the

Antelope Mask, from the Ivory Coast
From the Plass Collection

138

(*Anderson photograph*)   (*Anderson photograph*)

Venus de Medici   *Botticelli*, Detail, from Birth of Venus

Uffizi Gallery, Florence   *Uffizi Gallery, Florence*

cultural air he breathed, and that the cultural air of his generation can be confidently analysed and compared with that of the generation that produced the copy of a statue by Praxiteles.

There are plenty of more recent movements which we cannot yet see in perspective. The outburst of pseudo-African mannerisms which appeared in 1907, when Picasso and Braque caught fire at the sight of a carved figure from the Gold Coast, will seem sadly hollow when we know more about African art and are a little farther from the Parisian-African revival. Already Modigliani's Africanisms begin to look as sentimental as Victorian Elizabethanisms.

One of the characteristics of taste is that it is infectious. The essence of a mesh is that it is a repeating pattern, and although each repeat may depend for its shape on the operation of outside forces—economic, social, religious, political, climatic and so on—yet those forces can only operate on single individuals. And the particularly sensitive individuals who first respond to them become, themselves, forces that affect the whole surrounding area.

Whenever chroniclers attempt to explain the Zeitgeist, they fall back on phrases like "something in the air" or "opinions that spread imperceptibly from mind to mind". But that 'something' must have originated somewhere. The opinions must have been formed in individual minds—sometimes even in a single individual mind. Not until they have spread, like a fire, over a considerable area do they become recognisable as part of the spirit of an age or place. The speed at which they spread depends on the inflammability of the surrounding material; and the relative inflammability of different material is infinitely variable. Why was it impossible for the Gothic spark to ignite the upper classes of England in 1750? And why, a century later, had it consumed the whole country? Was it attributable to Wordsworth or the Oxford Movement or Ruskin? Are we to trace it farther back to Horace Walpole and Gray? Was it all these forces operating cumulatively in the same direction and producing a single force? Were those forces themselves the results of a "something in the air" that must be traced to an ever remoter origin? To the student of causes, the Zeitgeist is difficult to examine, because every cause becomes the effect of a remoter cause the moment he begins to examine it.

Once the fire has started, a new phase in the history of taste has begun. It is never possible to say at what point a number of individual consciousnesses become a group-consciousness. No one, for instance, can fix the date at which the temper of a handful of exceptional Italians produced the Italian Renaissance. The word 'Renaissance' is no more than the historian's recognition that the sieve was changing its mesh with unusual rapidity, and it is significant that the more closely historians study a given manifestation of the Zeitgeist, the earlier they place its origins.

Their attention is first attracted by its full flower, its completest and most spectacular manifestation. The Italian Renaissance begins by being synonymous, in the historian's mind, with the High Renaissance. The movement seemed to start with Leonardo and end with Tintoretto. But soon it becomes necessary to explain Leonardo. Research discovers the bud behind the flower, the stem behind the bud, and eventually the Renaissance is being traced to its roots in the Middle Ages. Sir Kenneth Clark's book on the Gothic Revival is a study of a movement that had a climax in the nineteenth century; but no sooner has the author begun to examine and account for the climax, than he is forced to point out that there is, in fact, no definite break between Gothic as the living (though moribund) expression of a mediæval frame of mind and Gothic as a dilettante's rediscovery of a dead language. Such admissions, always made by every serious writer who cuts off an arbitrary slice of the history of civilisation and puts it under the microscope, prove that it is impossible to think of taste as anything but a shifting pattern endlessly producing new combinations, endlessly responsive to the arrival of new influences, endlessly shaking off old ones.

But it is still necessary to establish a convenient starting-point; for the human mind in its journeyings is irritated by the absence of milestones. To-day the starting-point of the Italian Renaissance is not Leonardo but Giotto, and of Renaissance humanism not Marsilio Ficino or Alberti but St. Francis of Assisi. It still remains to explain how Giotto lit the spark which smouldered for one century and in the next set fire to the whole of North Italian thought and feeling; and it still remains to show why northern Italy was mildly hostile to such influences in the fourteenth century and susceptible to them in the fifteenth. "Something in the air" gave Giotto the clue to a new set of experiences in life and a new set of possibilities in art. That same 'something', reinforced by Giotto's example, made succeeding generations increasingly sensitive to the new possibilities. By the end of the fifteenth century it had become so pervasive that it no longer needed exceptional sensitivity to absorb it. It needed, in fact, exceptional obtuseness or conservatism to escape it. Once the Renaissance was in full flood, even the mediocre artist could achieve greatness. It is not by accident that at one moment of time only isolated genius is possible and at another great art can occur with frequency and ease. Potential genius crops up, by the law of averages, at the usual intervals throughout history, but only when environment is favourable can it flourish. The spirit of the age is created by the artist; but it also creates him.

The sieve of taste always rejects more than it transmits. It is difficult to realise how small a proportion of available experience is acceptable by a given stratum of society at a given time. If we draw the well-known distinction between sensation and perception—between what the senses present to the mind and what the mind can absorb from the senses—the percentage of sensations which we are capable of perceiving is negligible; this applies to all our perceptions, but particularly to aural and visual perceptions. What allows a sensation to become a perception is its capacity to *please*; or, to be more accurate, our capacity to be pleased by it. That, in its turn, is a function of our appetite, and our appetite, as has been suggested, leads us to call whatever gratifies it by the name of 'beautiful'. What passes through the sieve is, *ipso facto*, beautiful. The notion of 'taste' does not occur to the owner of the sieve, any more than the notion ever occurs to a man in love that the object of his affections is only desirable because his appetite of the moment happens to find her so. A generation that can only contemplate pointed arches and vertical rhythms with pleasure, and which views round arches and horizontal rhythms with distaste, is hardly conscious that it is only sensitive to an extremely limited set of visual experiences—that the number of curves and rhythms which can and do pass through its sieve is only a minute fraction of those that exist. It only knows, without troubling to ask why, that some forms are beautiful, some ugly and the majority negligible. It mistakes what is beautiful *to it* for absolute beauty, just as the lover mistakes the qualities of his beloved for absolute desirabilities. This limitation of our perceptions reduces the kind of experience that we are prepared to call 'beautiful' to a mere handful at any given time. But our attitude to the taste of the past, which we may understand but can never wholeheartedly share, is necessarily different from our attitude to the taste of our own day, which is an integral part of ourselves.

It is for that reason that the question of 'good taste' so easily arises when we come to consider contemporary manifestations of the Zeit-geist. Ardent and sensitive men whose judgment is in other respects balanced constantly feel an urge to point out the difference between good and bad design, good and bad sentiment, in the work of their immediate contemporaries. Alas, their contrasted pairs of teapots, chairs or refrigerators begin to tell a different story as soon as taste begins to change. Lantern-slides piously bequeathed to educational institutions by these apostles of good taste, in which the admirable and the abominable are set side by side, no longer point the moral they so aptly pointed twenty years ago. Indeed, if the donor has not troubled to label each photograph 'good' and 'bad', it is often impossible to guess which was which.

One can be fairly certain, when this happens, that the man who, only a few years ago, offered to discriminate between good taste and bad was not only the victim of his own taste—none of us can escape that—but was also in the clutches of that far more insidious phenomenon 'fashion'.

Fashion differs from taste in degree but not in kind. Its chief victims are not the artists who first seize on the "something in the air", but the sensitive, non-creative men who first take the infection from them. And its propagators are the second-rank artists who take their cue from the sensitive, non-creative men and produce a purified, half-sterilised version of the original impulse. Fashion differs from taste chiefly in its tempo—in the speed with which the meshes of the sieve react to the latest influence. And for that reason it gives us a far more detailed but far less generalised account of what is happening to our sense of beauty than does taste. It is rather like the seconds hand of a watch, which can split a minute into its component parts but cannot tell us the time of day.

Moreover, the pendulum of fashion not only swings faster than that of taste: it also swings more violently. Having decided that a particular quality is desirable, it exaggerates and isolates that quality and rejects all others. If simplicity is in vogue, then fashionable good taste will always prefer no ornament at all to simple ornament; if squareness is modish, even a teaspoon must be square; if suavity of line becomes desirable, then sloping shoulders come in and the ideal is a champagne bottle. The result of this extremism is that fashion sets up in the eye a mechanism of sheer boredom, and produces, automatically, revolutions that follow each other more rapidly than revolutions of taste. The fashionable of yesterday becomes the out-of-fashion of to-day more easily and more violently than can happen with the slower pendulum of taste. "In bad taste" is more likely to mean "out of fashion" than "a bad example of the fashionable".

But, precisely because 'fashion' moves more quickly and violently than taste, it provides a more convenient laboratory specimen for the observer. It is an easier phenomenon to examine at a given moment, and the evidence of its movements over a given period of time is more available. The passage, for example, from the Empire dress of 1800 to the full crinoline of 1840—from the body conceived as a column to the body conceived as a bell—could hardly have happened in so short a time in the history of the fine arts. Every step in the transition can be accurately observed in the fashion plates of the period. No wonder the students of the Zeitgeist have chosen fashion rather than taste as their subject.

In particular it provides revealing evidence about the process of infection by means of which both taste and fashion spread. The original creative artist, to whom all manifestations of taste can be ultimately traced, transmits his influence first to the sensitive, non-creative man already mentioned, from whom it is caught by the secondary derivative artist, who, in his turn, transmits it by means of manufactured articles and minor works of art to the strata of society most susceptible to it. It appears, first of all, in the kind of manufactured articles which need the least amount of readjustment in methods of manufacture; textiles and wallpapers catch it before furniture and cutlery. The wall paper with a cubist basis of design appears at a shorter interval after the first cubist paintings than do the starkly angular chairs or the spoons with a rectangular bowl. But in the end, and at different intervals, dependent on the amount of dislocation caused by the change over, the whole visual background to life is altered, from the house that changes its pitched roof for a flat one to the table that supports a cactus instead of a Chinese vase.

The initial demand is small and prices correspondingly high. Once the demand has been started by the small original group, it spreads first to the moderately rich intellectual—'moderately' because the very rich are usually well provided with possessions whose expensiveness depends on rarity rather than on novelty. Just as a Titian is less easy to replace by a Picasso than is a Manet, so the Chippendale sideboard is less easy to replace than the sideboard that is only just outmoded. The contagion then spreads downwards at speeds governed by the income and the mental adaptability of the social strata through which it passes, and their geographical distance from the original radiating-point. Similar social strata feel the impact earlier in Paris than in London, earlier in London than in Manchester. Eventually it permeates the whole of society within the area susceptible to infection, for the world is not yet a single cultural unit and there are still plenty of areas outside the range of European influence.

At present the complete process of infection from start to finish—from the removal of the first aspidistra to the extinction of the whole species—occupies something like a quarter of a century. And the innate human conservatism, which acts as a brake on the early stages of it, actually accelerates it in its later stages. Once the cactus has outnumbered the aspidistra, the normal man's hatred of making himself conspicuous by belonging to a minority will certainly cause a sharp rise in the mortality rate of aspidistras. A study of the window curtains and of the ornaments visible behind them on a walk from Chelsea to Shoreditch would reveal specimens at every stage in the downward progress of fashion.

But is it possible to apply the word 'bad' in an absolute sense to particular manifestations of fashion? In any enquiry which envisages beauty as an absolute value, that must be the central, the inescapable question. The division, insisted on with such assurance to-day, of design into 'good' and 'bad' implies a standard. It also implies an unchanging standard. It would be useless to apply tests to design in the twentieth century which were not equally valid when applied to design in any other century. It is foolish, for example, to speak of 'good, simple shapes' (with the implication that simplicity is an absolute virtue and that goodness and simplicity are synonymous), when we know that many past ages have produced complicated shapes, and that they, too, have been good. Admitting that we are all at the mercy of an æsthetic censorship which, at any given moment and in any given social stratum, can only admit one *kind* of beauty, is it not possible that of two given objects one is *better of its kind* than the other? Of course, there is such a thing as 'bad', both functionally and æsthetically. And, of course, there is a purpose to be served by those organisations, like the Design Council or the Design and Industries Association, that exist to encourage 'good design' on the part of artists and 'good taste' on the part of the public. But I doubt whether they have a clear notion of what their purpose is or of how to put it into effect.

Presumably chosen from the 'moderately rich intellectual' stratum, their job, as they envisage it, is to accelerate the process of contagion and to see to it that fashion spreads with the utmost possible speed. If it has been decided that aspidistras are 'bad', then it becomes their duty to preach against aspidistras until an obedient public has banished the last offending specimen from their homes. That the plant ever found its way into their homes can only be explained in one of two ways. Either it was always 'bad' but nobody realised it because nobody had, till now, been admitted to the secret of 'good taste'. Or else it was once good and has only recently *become* bad because of the advent of a new set of æsthetic tests—tests no more valid than the old ones, but more acceptable because more up-to-date.

The illusion that the gift of 'good taste' was withheld from the preceding generation, but granted to a few enlightened members of the generation to which we belong, is a useful one. It would certainly damp the enthusiasm of the prophets of good taste if they realised that they were, in fact, victims of an illusion; it would take the heart out of their championship of the up-to-date and blunt the edge of their scorn for the out-of-date. Both enthusiasm and scorn are indispensable motive forces. Without them the wheels of change would certainly move at a slower pace. And without change we should drift into a fatal apathy. But though change is necessary for development, it is certainly not synonymous with 'improvement', and if the phenomenon of taste is to be viewed objectively, it is necessary to point out that illusion plays its part.

Instances of this particular illusion are not difficult to find in the past. Here, for example, is one instructive passage from a series of lectures on interior decoration delivered under the auspices of the

Royal Society of Arts by an eminent and extremely progressive architect in 1881:

"I can conceive nothing more terrible than to be doomed to spend one's life in a house furnished after the fashion of twenty years ago." This is passionate language, and one would expect it to be followed by a convincing attack on the fashions of 1861. The attack certainly develops and at some length. It makes instructive reading, but it is certainly not convincing. "Dull, monotonous walls," says Professor Edis, "on which garish flock papers of the vulgarest possible design stare one blankly in the face." No reasoned attack could complain in the same sentence of dullness and garishness, of monotonous blankness and vulgar over-emphasis. But the professor is not conducting a reasoned attack. Both he and his audience are in the grip of a powerful æsthetic emotion, and as long as his words convey the emotion he can carry his audience with him.

His enthusiasm for 1881 is pitched in the same passionate key as his scorn of 1861. "In this æsthetic age, when there is a general demand for greater beauty, when we are getting rid of the vile old willow pattern, when grates and fenders, chairs and couches must be designed in conformity with the dictates of an elevated taste" is a heartening phrase, but there is no attempt to explain why willow pattern should be vile because it is old, or what is the real difference between the dictates of elevated and debased taste. Whenever he quotes specific instances, the professor is apt to contradict himself. Floral ornament, for example, if it occurs in 1861, is referred to as "silly representations of vegetable life"; if it is contemporary, it is admirable, and young ladies should be encouraged to produce it. "Good taste, which most educated ladies possess, will suggest many ways of adapting flowers of the field in proper decorative treatment."

We read sentiments like these with cynical amusement. Professor Edis's sieve has a different mesh from ours, and we know that only an audience with a set of tastes similar to his own can grasp his meaning. For it is a meaning based on a set of standards that we have long since abandoned. We know that there was a difference between 1861 and 1881, but we cannot see it as a chasm with 'the vulgarest possible design' on one side and 'elevated taste' on the other. Unlike the philosophers' books on æsthetics, Professor Edis's lectures are copiously illustrated. We are shown exactly what he had in mind when he spoke of 'elevated taste', but what appeared to Professor Edis as a change from vulgar to elevated taste seems to us no more than a change from heavy to lighter forms. And we may be quite sure that our own complacent sense of the chasm between the taste of our own day and that of twenty years ago will give rise to the same kind of cynical amusement a hundred years hence.

But it does not follow that because of this illusion—this natural love of the up-to-date and impatience with the out-of-date—there is no such thing as good and bad in æsthetic judgment. It has already been pointed out (p. 144) that the phrase "in bad taste", in the mouth of a contemporary, is more likely to mean "out of fashion" than "a bad example of the fashionable". But bad examples of the fashionable do exist, and the test for them is simple.

If, as has been so often repeated in this book, the basis of art is love and the basis of Nature efficiency, then the test of 'goodness' in art is the depth and intensity of the artist's love, and the test of 'goodness' in Nature is the extent of her efficiency. Being part of Nature's plan, we human beings are not in a position to judge her efficiency, but we do, at least, know that many of Nature's experiments have been abandoned as being inefficient. Nature has her own dustbin into which her failures disappear; and the only instances of natural 'badness' we normally encounter occur when two attempts at efficiency collide and damage each other. Perhaps if we could take a longer view of the evolutionary forces, we should not be quite so sure that a leaf half eaten by a caterpillar is an example of 'badness' in leaves, or that a caterpillar that was undernourished because of its failure to eat sufficient leaves is an example of 'badness' in caterpillars. Being incapable of taking the long view, it does seem to us that when function is interfered with 'badness' results.

It is worth noting, by the way, that certain man-made objects have been constructed on Nature's plan. A scythe owes its shape entirely to its efficiency. Love has played no part in its designing. Any conscious attempt to give it beauty would, in some way, mar its effectiveness. The curve of the handle and the blade could only be 'improved' in the direction of making it a more efficient tool for cutting long grass. But such purely functional man-made objects are very rare. Even the most utilitarian of household appliances, such as tablespoons or sauce-pans, have a conscious æsthetic element in them. It is customary for designers to boast that the latest shape is more efficient than its pre-decessor, but I suspect that fashionable shape plays a greater part than the designer will admit—or than he even consciously knows; and that a love of streamlining is just as potent as a desire for efficiency when the industrial designer makes his first sketch for a refrigerator or an electric-iron.

But if badness in Nature is a failure of function, badness in art is largely a failure of love. That is the only possible test, and if it were as easy to judge love as it is to judge efficiency, fewer mistakes would be made by critics, and the endless disputes about good and bad taste would resolve themselves into a simple set of admissions. "This work of art is the product of a set of loves which I cannot share: therefore I cannot be moved by it." "This artist has so completely translated my own loves into visible terms that I am entranced by his painting." Such admissions would clear away the kind of misconceptions that are based on differences in the kind of thing loved, and would leave our judgment free to examine the real roots of 'good' and 'bad' which can only be traced to different intensities of love, or even of false or simulated love.

Taken in this sense, the phrases 'good taste' and 'bad taste' involve two variable quantities—the goodness or badness of the work of art judged ("it *is in* bad taste") and the sensitivity, developed or undeveloped, of the judge ("he *has* bad taste"). The different inten-sities of love that give rise to work of different degrees of 'goodness' have already been touched on in the last chapter. Here we are con-cerned with the capacity of the judge to recognise such differences of degree. And only a developed sensitivity can be trusted to distinguish between them. In this sense and in no other has the phrase 'good taste' any meaning.

CHAPTER IX

'Good Taste'

L UCKILY FOR THE ROUGH-AND-READY DECISIONS OF EVERYDAY
life, but unluckily for our judgment of artists, there are no
infallible tests for the intensity or the genuineness of love.
Posterity arrives at unquestionable decisions about the art of the
distant past. The accumulated weight of sensitive opinion about Old
Masters *is* infallible, and those of us who cannot, in our heart of hearts,
agree with any specific judgment of posterity can only blame our own
limited capacity for understanding. But with the art of the present and
the immediate past, the case is very different.

As I write I am sitting on a spur of the South Downs, overlooking
an immense fertile plain stretching northwards into a blue distance.
A quarter of a mile away is a freshly cut cornfield. A hundred artists
have tackled such a theme memorably; and thousands have tackled it
unmemorably, captivated by what they would call its beauty, but
failing to persuade the spectator that what they had done was worth
doing; and certainly not always failing through lack of technical
skill.

Among memorable interpretations of such a scene—landscapes by
Brueghel, Turner, Constable, Linnell, Monet, van Gogh and Dufy
occur to me—all of them (with the possible exception of Constable's)
less *like* what I think I see than many of the mediocre landscapes that
fail to interest me. Asked to explain why this should be so, I can glibly
reply that the great landscape artists have something called 'vision'
denied to lesser men, and that I have something called 'good taste'
which enables me to recognise and enjoy their vision. I can add, even
more glibly, that 'vision' penetrates beyond mere optical experience,
and that if an accurate documentary account of the landscape before
my eyes is all that is required of a work of art, then the camera can do

Linnell, Noonday Rest

Tate Gallery, London

Dufy, Cornfield

Van Gogh, Cornfield

Gemente Museum, Amsterdam

the job as well as, though no better than, a skilful painter. But such explanations are too superficial to be satisfactory.

The nature of vision has been dealt with at some length already. Briefly, it is an emotionalised attitude of mind, a set of enthusiasms and boredoms, which can only find expression in visual terms. 'Good taste' is therefore a receptive attitude of mind which works backwards through the artist's visual expression to his vision. It is, in fact, nothing more than the capacity to understand the work of art, and, by understanding it, to share the particular kind of love that was responsible for its creation. Only in so far as the spectator can share the artist's emotion can his taste be described as 'good'. But, having shared it, he can then pass judgment on it. He can recognise, for example, though he cannot prove, that van Gogh's love of certain aspects of a cornfield was more intense than Linnell's love of a different set of aspects. And that, though their 'styles' are different, because each has fastened on a

(*Anderson photograph*)

Michelangelo, Adam. Detail from the ceiling of the Sistine Chapel, Rome

Bronzino, detail from fresco
Church of San Lorenzo, Florence

different aspect of cornfieldness, they can still be compared. If I find Linnell's attitude to cornfields more sympathetic to me than van Gogh's, that reveals no more than a certain compatibility of temperament between myself and the artist. But that has nothing to do with the intensity of his attitude. And if I find myself forced to admit that though Linnell may be more congenial to me, which is a subjective judgment, van Gogh's statement is more passionate, more confident, more single-hearted, which is an objective judgment, then I must also admit that van Gogh is the greater artist of the two.

In such a case I can only conclude that my taste is bad. I have failed to prefer the greater to the lesser. I am capable of sharing the lesser emotion but not the greater; my subjective and objective judgments are in conflict, and therefore complete understanding is impossible.

At this point it becomes necessary to look rather more closely into the difference between taste and fashion. Taste I have already defined as the capacity to understand and to share the emotional impulse of the artist. And when the artist lived centuries ago, there is little difficulty

153

in doing so. Whatever was ephemeral or topical in the work of art has long since evaporated. In 1512 the Sistine Chapel ceiling seemed to the cultivated Roman astonishing because it was entirely new. No artist had ever conceived the human body in those terms before. It was magnificent, certainly, but its chief effect must have been not of magnificence but of unfamiliarity. Indeed, so remarkable was the impact of it, that it set a fashion which persisted for a whole century—a fashion for muscular sublimity which can be traced in a hundred tiresome little tricks—the bent wrist, the detached forefinger, the twisted torso and so on. Under the spell of that fashion it must have seemed that Michelangelo's Mannerist followers had outdone their master. Vasari, Bronzino, Pontormo and the rest did all that Michelangelo had done, and did it even more thoroughly.

Now a certain percentage of unfamiliarity has already been postulated as a necessary ingredient in beauty, and with Michelangelo the percentage is unusually high. Even to-day, familiar though we are with the Michelangelesque *terribilità*, we cannot fail to realise it. But we can no longer realise it *as a fashion*; it is no longer topical or delightful by virtue of its newness. On the contrary, it has passed into the currency of our taste. The disturbing enthusiasms and hatreds that always attach themselves to fashion have been left behind, and nothing remains but the permanent values. We see Michelangelo as a man who originated an attitude to the human body because he loved with such extraordinary intensity its muscular virility and flexibility. And we see Vasari and Bronzino as rather ridiculous apes, men in the grip of a fashion, and therefore unable to distinguish between the true and the false. The writhing torsos of their frescoes are the equivalent of the spoons that became rectangular in the interests of the Cubist fashion of the twenties of our own century.

But though we find it easy to apply to the fifteenth and sixteenth centuries the infallible tests of taste, when we come to the nineteenth and twentieth we are victims of the extremely fallible pressure of fashion. We are no more capable of comparing Linnell with van Gogh than Vasari was of comparing Pollaiuolo with Michelangelo. We think we are looking for different degrees of artistic merit, but what we actually see are different degrees of familiarity. Van Gogh has produced something new, and merely because it is new we are almost incapable of

(*By courtesy of Mrs. Lowinski*)

Samuel Palmer, Cornfield

knowing whether it is good. We only know that it was, until quite recently, extremely fashionable, and that we are now watching it slowly become outmoded.

Linnell *has* become outmoded. He is still subject to the laws of fashion. He has not yet reached the point when we can judge him by the solider, slower tempo of the laws of taste. For fashion has two phases—a positive, in which we are passionately interested either for or against according to the degree of conservatism with which we approach the new, and a negative phase, in which we are still passionately concerned, but towards which we are instinctively hostile because it is the opposite of new. It is dowdy. If it were bad we could forget it; but it is outmoded and we cannot forgive it. In the domain of taste we are no longer concerned with newness or the reverse.

One of the most interesting phenomena in the study of taste is the emergence from dowdiness of one artist after another. Samuel Palmer for example, ignored for half a century as a minor nineteenth-century romantic, has just emerged. The final verdict on him has not yet been passed. There is a tendency to exaggerate his virtues. He is fêted by his discoverers like a man just released from prison: his connection with Blake has given him a slightly inflated value. But his furious romanticism and the strange mood of pastoral tranquillity he often achieved endear him to the present generation.

Linnell is beginning to catch a little reflected light from Palmer. Perhaps ten years ago his name would not have been included in my list of the men who have painted cornfields memorably. But to-day one recognises, with a slight shock of surprise, an echo in his landscapes of that same pastoral warmth, that affection for lush growth, that makes Samuel Palmer attractive. He, too, has lifted a corner of the veil that hangs between the seen world and the felt. That is not a careless phrase. I believe it to be an exact description—as far as any metaphor can be exact—of the artist's creative process. The world of the eye and the world of the mind are equally important and equally valid, even though the former can be measured and the latter cannot. Artists have always varied in the extent to which they could move easily and confidently in one or the other. A Blake feels himself at home in the world of the mind, a Velazquez in the world of the eye, but neither would be an artist at all if both worlds were not available to them. Between the two worlds hangs a veil which the artist must always try to lift and the scientist never.

"Don't brood too much," wrote Margaret Schlegel to her sister Helen in E. M. Forster's *Howard's End*—"don't brood too much on the superiority of the unseen to the seen. It's true: but to brood on it is mediæval. Our business is not to contrast the two but to reconcile them."

The world of the senses, measurable though it is, is meaningless unless that reconciliation has been made, and only the artist can make it. The world of the mind is non-existent unless it has been approached by way of the senses. This sounds rather like the Platonic theory of the real and the ideal, but it is, in fact, the exact reverse of Platonism. I much prefer to regard 'reality' as a set of phenomena which await the interpretation of each separate individual, than as a set of shadows cast on a screen by a hidden but even more 'real' world which we cannot see but must always deduce by watching the behaviour of the shadows. Both conceptions are, in any case, no more than metaphors, and both involve the idea of a veil hanging between the ponderable and the imponderable—between the scientist's world of fact and the artist's world of value.

The ability to lift this veil is the secret of 'vision'. Without it all art is useless, though it may, for a time, be fashionable. It matters little whether the painter is a realist like Velazquez or a formalist like Picasso. He may interpret the unseen in terms of the seen, or he may attempt to create a painterly equivalent of the unseen. In the long run, posterity will judge him, not by his method, but by the completeness with which he expresses his inner life. The veil is always there, and the innumerable mediocrities who cannot lift it will always leave us unmoved. They cannot enlarge *our* lives, because there is nothing in *their* lives that was not already in our own. All we can do is to admire their craftsmanship, their skill in presenting us with something of which we have no need.

But the nearer we come to our own time, the less we are able to recognise what it is that is being presented to us. Our understanding of art depends to a surprising extent on our cumulative experience of it. Once a fragment of the veil has been lifted, it has been lifted for ever. That particular fragment of the seen has been reconciled with the unseen, and for the whole of posterity it will, to repeat my own phrase, "never be the same again".

The artists of the past who have lifted the veil have had plenty of time for their 'reconciliations' of the seen and the unseen to become familiar to us. Their interpretations of life have passed into currency. They are authentic and convincing. We easily see the human body in terms of the Michelangelesque, the Titianesque, the Rubensesque, the Renoiresque. All these attitudes of mind, which were once remarkable discoveries, are now commonplaces. We may not find them all equally congenial, but they are all equally convincing. But the artist who has only just begun to twitch away *his* corner of the veil is revealing something we have never seen before. His work contains so large a percentage of the unfamiliar that we cannot possibly accept it as valid. Posterity has, as yet, made no pronouncement on it. The sieve of our own taste will not allow it to pass through the mesh.

I do not mean that each artist reveals an entirely new world of his own. Even the most daring originators cannot help basing themselves largely on tradition.

There seems to be a definite limit set to the amount of new matter that any artist can inject into the tradition of his time. And the most curious feature of this limit is that it is not imposed by the artist's lack of inventiveness, but by his sense of fitness—one might almost say his sense of artistic decency. We have few records of the purely inventive processes that every artist must indulge in as he ruminates about the *possibilities* of his art. Artists are not averse to theorising, and their theories usually make tiresome reading, for their works of art either confirm their theories, thereby rendering them superfluous, or contradict them, thereby making them meaningless. But their theories almost always concern the pictures they are going to paint, whereas, if ever an artist dares to contemplate the full possibilities of his art, he is bound to envisage works of art which he will never produce.

One of the few artists who have left records of this kind of speculation was Leonardo, whose mind, unlike that of almost any artist known to us, alternated between purely intellectual speculation and creative imagination. And it is noteworthy that the speculative side of Leonardo's mind constantly provoked him to imagine pictures which his creative side had no intention of producing. His researches into the "perspective of colour" are penetrating, and if he had carried them into effect he would have painted pictures far closer to Impressionism than his creative side dared attempt. One passage in the *Trattato della Pittura* anticipates Rembrandt. He describes the 'charm' of a person sitting in a doorway against a dark background, with one half of the face "lost in the darkness of the house". Now Leonardo certainly carried, not only the study but the painting of chiaroscuro farther than any of his contemporaries, but his 'taste'—his sense of fitness—would never have allowed him to 'lose' a contour in a shadow, though his logical mind could see that contours are frequently so lost, and though his whole theory of painting was a plea for realism.

It seems that in all artists a sense of the artistic decencies, as evolved by generations and hallowed by the gradual growth of tradition, is at war with their sense of the artistic possibilities. And in this conflict the whole weight of fashion is on the side of established convention.

There is no reason why a man should not dress in any fashion he admires, and it would be an uphill task to prove that Elizabethan clothes were not, in an absolute sense, more 'beautiful' than those of our own day. Yet no man dares to obey his sense of beauty rather than his sense of fashion (his 'dislike', as he would call it, 'of making himself conspicuous'). One would have expected the artist, at least, to be content to be conspicuous in the interests of beauty.

The extent to which the visual arts insist on borrowing from tradition is startling. One would have thought, for example, that architecture, which is largely an abstract art and whose only limitations of form are those dictated by function (columns must support weight, doors must be large enough to admit a human being, windows must be spaced in the interests of light and ventilation), would have evolved a bewildering multiplicity of styles. There is no difficulty in *imagining* a hundred different forms of column and capital. Yet ever since the Italian Renaissance became conscious of Classic architecture, architects have insisted on making themselves abject slaves to the laws laid down by Vitruvius. The Bank of England, which should surely be the outward manifestation of a nineteenth-century outlook, copies meticulously forms that were evolved by the Greeks in the fifth century B.C. (themselves slavish stone versions of wooden buildings evolved centuries earlier) and have been repeated with parrot-like fidelity ever since the early fifteenth century. There are more Ionic columns supporting the Georgian porticoes of London than in the whole of Greece.

The reason why artists are not more inventive is not that they cannot invent but that they feel it indecent to do so. Their inventions would somehow lack sanction. The Chinese sage who, after reading a poem which broke the time-honoured canons of poetry, said, "There is no such poem", uttered a profound truth. For tradition forms habit-tracks in the mind, appetites and disgusts which are the exact equivalents of the appetites and disgusts founded on our experience of Nature and which establish our standards of beauty. An architect familiar with ornament based on the vine or the acanthus would certainly have no difficulty in *imagining* ornament based on the sweet pea or the dandelion. But having, so to speak, offered the new motive to his own mind, he would find himself unable to accept its validity owing to the absence of habit-tracks along which it could move easily.

It is interesting to note that a follower of Brunelleschi did, in fact, introduce an ornamental motive based on the pea-pod into the dome of the Cathedral of Florence, but banished it to the cupola, where it looks surprisingly ill at ease now that modern photography has made it easily available.

(*By courtesy of J. M. Dent & Sons, Ltd.*)
Beardsley, Design for cover of 'Le Morte d'Arthur'

Occasional daring attempts have been made to enlarge the decorative repertory of the designer, but fashion, after giving them a short-lived welcome, has ultimately rejected them in its negative phase before they could produce habit-tracks. The sunflower motives of the eighties, the outburst of Iceland poppies that made its appearance with *art nouveau* in the first decade of this century, have never passed into general currency.

In consciously Classic periods of taste—in mid-seventeenth-century

France, for example—this adherence to traditional form becomes a major item in the artistic creed: the Classic artist is proud of his refusal to recognise new currency. But even in periods notable for their inventiveness, an involuntary brake holds the artist back. Even in moments when the artist is, to all appearances, frankly engaged in a struggle for complete realism, his progress towards it is automatically retarded. There is no reason to suppose that the carvers of the archaic Greek adolescents of the sixth century B.C. were not anxious to produce something as natural, as 'real', as Praxiteles; nor did any limitation in their technical equipment prevent them from doing so. What did prevent them was largely a sense that a Praxitelean statue would have looked 'wrong'. The well-developed naked human body was familiar enough to their eyes, but it had no ancestry in art. Its interpretation in sculpture did not yet exist. Therefore it had no artistic validity. Only after two centuries of inch-by-inch progress could the predestined Praxitelean idiom be achieved. In that progress the individual contribution of each separate sculptor was negligible, yet each of them would, if questioned as to his ideal statue, have described something that sounded rather Praxitelean.

Leonardo, without even the spur of a question, did describe pictures that sound Caravaggian or Rembrandtian, but he was only able to paint pictures which, however charged with his personal temperament, were Verrocchian in idiom.

The reason why every artist finds his memory-images of other men's works of art so much more potent than his memory-images of life as observed by himself sheds a good deal of light on the nature of art. Life produces a vast stock of visual experience, but since all of it belongs to the world of action, it is difficult to isolate it as *pure* visual experience. The work of art, on the other hand, exists only to be contemplated, and therefore bites deeper into the visual memory. A real leaf can be smelled, touched, even eaten, as well as contemplated. And even as an object to be contemplated it changes its appearance with every gust of wind, every variation of light, every angle of vision. The painted or carved leaf is static and consequently memorable. Moreover, if the carved or painted leaf is by a contemporary or near-contemporary, it will have all the fashionable qualities that will make it acceptable. It will, in fact, be an extract from Nature's leaf, and what has been extracted will be precisely what the artist is unconsciously looking for. Consciously he would say that *his* leaf is taken direct from Nature. Unconsciously he can only find in Nature what his predecessors have already found, plus a surprisingly small contribution of his own. Extraordinary instances of the influence of art upon artists, and the

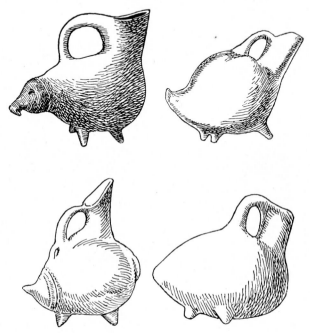

(*From Evans, 'The Palace of Minos', by permission of the author's executors and Macmillan & Co. Ltd.*)

Four Cretan Pot Vessels from the Palace of Minos, Crete

almost negligible influence of life, can be found among the crafts. For example, a series of Cretan pot vessels belonging to the Middle Minoan period, discovered by Sir Arthur Evans, vary a good deal in size and proportion, but are all alike in that they have a snout at one end, a sharp point at the other and four legs on the underside. It is obvious that those which most nearly resemble the form of a pig have been copied from wineskins made of the skin of a pig. There is no ritual or other reason for their shape than this. Wine was carried in containers of recognisably pig-like form, consequently the form is kept though the reason for it has vanished. Later, these pig-shaped vessels lost a good deal of their resemblance to the prototype by being copied from each other rather than from the original skin.

If art were based entirely on the artist's observation and invention, the word 'tradition' would have no meaning. But without a minimum of observation and invention—the amount of which varies from period to period—tradition would be incapable of development.

Looking back through art history and regarding it as a continuous pattern of development, we can see at a glance exactly which elements in an artist's work were taken from his predecessors and which were his own original contributions. But when we come to the artists of our own time, the laws of taste become superseded by the laws of fashion. Fashion allows us to be pleased only with what is modish and accepted. Whatever, in a contemporary artist's work, springs naturally from contemporary tradition, we take so completely for granted that it becomes invisible. Whatever is entirely his own, and has therefore not yet had time to insinuate itself into the currently accepted idiom, must of necessity be puzzling at the moment of its first appearance. And as long as it remains puzzling, it must be rejected. Only by a comparatively slow and rather mysterious process does it establish its claim to validity. And having done so, it modifies the fashion-formula and sets up in us a new set of æsthetic appetites. In this way the fashion-formula develops, continually adding new elements to its head, continually shedding them from its tail. And as the discarded elements free themselves from the fashion-formula, they come under the more discriminating, less ephemeral laws of taste, and either disappear as being worthless or else help to form a new link in the chain of established tradition.

The process whereby each new lifting of the veil manages at length to persuade us of its sincerity and validity certainly is mysterious. It is a fairly common phenomenon in my own experience to find that the considerable shock of surprise and discomfort at encountering for the first time a new revelation by a contemporary or an unfamiliar artist is modified at the second encounter, especially if a period of time has elapsed between the two encounters. I have noticed this particularly with the, to me, less familiar art of music. What seemed to me baffling and lacking in inevitability at the first hearing began to achieve meaning and coherence at the second, even though no conscious process of disentanglement or even of recollection had taken place in the interval. Some curious mechanism of unconscious digestion enables us to adapt ourselves to the unfamiliar, and to absorb it without expenditure of effort, though not without expenditure of time.

The perfectly natural hostility which every normal man feels in face of the unfamiliar—long before he has asked himself whether it is a genuine revelation or a piece of charlatanism—is a commonplace of art history. Instances of it can be found wherever one consults the records of contemporary comment. There is an impression that it is a comparatively recent growth, that it began with the nineteenth century, and has intensified itself until to-day we automatically assume that the artist who is attacked on the grounds of unintelligibility is almost certain to be acclaimed as a genius to-morrow. That impression is partly due to the fact that art criticism is a comparatively recent growth, and that critics before the nineteenth century did not so freely commit their hostility to writing. But there is, I think, another reason. The misunderstood genius really is a particularly characteristic figure of the last hundred years. He is a product of the romantic age, and in order to explain him it will be necessary to examine the nature of Romanticism itself.

In the chapter on Art and again in the discussion of Veronese's picture, I pointed out that form and content are so closely interrelated that only when the one finds its counterpart in the other can the work of art strike with its full force. But content, in the sense of the artist's emotional attitude, the precise flavour of the comment he wants to make, must *dictate* form. It can never have its full effect if it is poured into a ready-made form. Consequently as the flavour changes, as change it must with the passage of time and the evolution of civilisation, adjustments must continually be made in the accepted form-convention.

But in periods where unusually rapid changes are taking place in the emotional flavour, there occurs an inevitable time-lag. Form cannot catch up with content, and one of two things must happen. Either the artist tries to fit the new message into an outmoded form, and the result is an anachronism. Or he wildly experiments with new forms in the hope of finding an appropriate means of expressing his vision. The result is what is known as Romanticism.

Romanticism in art is necessarily a temporary phase. It can only last as long as some new emotional urge has rendered old forms obsolete. As soon as a new and satisfactory form-convention has been found to contain it, Classicism can resume its sway. The theorist again comes into his own: the formula hardens and sets, and remains set until a further change of heart again renders it obsolete.

Naturally the rhythm of this alternating domination of form and content is a slow one, and the moments when the two are perfectly adjusted to each other are brief. They are the periods that everyone admires. But the intervening periods split taste into two camps. Devotees of law, clarity and reason admire the periods when form is dominant and the artist in whom it is dominant. Those who demand from the artist a 'message' rather than a satisfying embodiment of a message are happiest with the emotional, experimental phase.

Each of the arts provides clear-cut instances of both phases. It is obvious, for example, that to Racine clarity of form, the utmost precision in the placing of dramatic climaxes, the strict observance of the dramatic unities of time and place, the unbroken beat of the Alexandrine line, all these formal elements are of the utmost importance. The ideal form has been discovered. Literary classicism has become crystallised, and Racine would rather weaken the impact of his emotional message than break so perfect a mould.

It is equally obvious that Shakespeare will break any mould that interferes with his message. Clarity, law, the placing of climaxes, unity of mood, the regular beat of the iambic pentameter, are unimportant as compared with his total content.

Bach and Wagner, Ghiberti and Rodin, Claude and Turner, the Parthenon and Chartres Cathedral, can all be contrasted with each other in the same way. But they are not opposites in the sense that the North and the South Poles are opposite. They are opposites in the sense that both poles are opposed to the centre of the earth, or as a point on the circumference of a wheel is opposed to its centre. The romantic is centrifugal, restless, capable of taking any direction provided it leads away from the norm. Above all, he is an individualist. The classic is centripetal, static, law-abiding; he is obsessed by the norm; he suppresses his individuality.

The whole subject is fascinating, and it has never been satisfactorily examined in all its strange ramifications, though a great deal of propagandist and overheated literature has gathered round the struggle between the two since the French Academy of the seventeenth century exhausted itself in futile argument on the relative merits of Poussin and Rubens. It is not my intention to add to that literature now. My only reason for this highly simplified digression is that it provides an explanation for the phenomenon of the misunderstood genius, and for the failure, at certain periods, of contemporary taste to recognise this "lifting of the veil" as a genuine manifestation of art.

The very conception of genius is a romantic one. In classic and post-classic periods the test of the artist's greatness is his power to make satisfactory use of familiar, accepted forms. New though his content may occasionally be, the syntax and the vocabulary he uses are never puzzling. He may make strides, but they are strides in a familiar direction. Contemporary taste is never in any doubt as to his worth, for his achievement differs chiefly in degree and hardly at all in kind from that of his predecessors. He may add to the tradition of his age, but he does not rebel against it. In romantic periods, on the other hand, it is the rebel, the individualist, who dominates, and his attempt to create new forms, new techniques, revolutionary types of syntax, daring additions to the vocabulary, are bound to be puzzling. The innovations he makes are bound to seem destructive, for they always jettison the familiar vessel in their attempt to create a new one to hold the new content. The conservative concludes that his leg is being pulled, and persists in so thinking until the new form, by dint of repetition, has established itself. Once it has done so, a new era of Classicism is on the way.

It follows that the phenomenon of the misunderstood genius occurs usually in periods when a new kind of content has forced the artist to abandon the old form, and an extreme example of such a period is our own.

When the art historian of the future looks back over the course of art evolution, he will certainly see the beginning of the twentieth century as one of its major turning-points. There have been others. The official recognition of Christianity in the fourth century A.D.

marked one of them; the impact of Renaissance humanism in Italy at the beginning of the fifteenth was another. Each of these moments had its own motive force drawn from utterly different sources. The turning-point from Pagan to Christian art depended on a new emphasis on a set of mystical values incomprehensible to Paganism. The Renaissance had its roots in a belief in the individual and in his power to understand and interpret his physical environment. But in both cases the effect on art was the same. In both cases the change followed the same pattern.

(Anderson photograph)

Good Shepherd Mosaic
Mausoleum of Galla Placidia, Ravenna

It was a search for new forms based on an unsuccessful attempt to use the old. And during the search art became temporarily split into two camps, of which the old, the familiar, was incapable of carrying the burden of the new message, while the new was not yet sufficiently consolidated to do it justice.

Thus the earliest Byzantine imagery (the 'Good Shepherd' mosaic in the mausoleum of Galla Placidia in Ravenna is a fair example) attempts to clothe itself in Pagan garments—no other garments being available—and fails to make itself explicit. "Jesus or Apollo?" we ask, for the beardless figure is neither physically perfect enough to satisfy the Pagan nor spiritual enough to satisfy the Christian. But gradually, after an uneasy transitional period with many borrowings from the Orient and many discardings and reshapings of Western idioms, the Byzantine style evolved, and proved in the end so satisfactory a medium of expression that it continued, virtually unchanged, until the Renaissance rendered it obsolete.

(*Anderson photograph*)

Duccio, Christ Appearing to the Apostles

Siena Cathedral

The Renaissance, too, had its period of uneasy transition. In certain panels in Duccio's Maiestà, side by side with figures that attempt the new volume and solidity, are figures that are completely symbolic, hieratic and two-dimensional. Giotto, working at the same time and introducing more genuinely original matter into his art than any other single figure in the whole history of painting, laid the foundations of Renaissance humanism, but even a century later the problem of consolidating the new style had not been solved. Masaccio was groping magnificently forward towards the triumph of individualism, while Fra Angelico was looking radiantly backwards at the mediæval world.

We have few records of contemporary opinion about these cleavages, though one suspects that the practising artist was usually on the side of the new, and the layman—so far as he had an opinion—on the side of the old. But in any case the new was bound to win. The artists of a hundred years later were studying the Masaccio frescoes in the Brancacci chapel with an almost reverent fervour, while the Fra Angelico frescoes at San Marco had surprisingly little influence. They were marvellous anachronisms, and only an artistic genius with a mediæval mind could have produced them. Benozzo Gozzoli, who adopted his master's mannerisms, was no genius and had a typically Renaissance mind. The best he could do with Fra Angelico's influence was to evolve a style that had neither the radiant mysticism of the Middle Ages nor the confident solidity of the Renaissance. He was a misfit, and his highest achievement—the 'Journey of the Magi' in the Riccardi chapel—is no more than joyful decoration.

Art to-day is again split into two camps, but split more violently than ever before. To-day old forms persist, anachronistically, by the side of new ones; we have by this time passed through the period in which new ideas attempted to use existing idioms. Both Cézanne and van Gogh began by adopting a purely Impressionist technique. Both used it without conviction, for their hearts were not in the Impressionist search for visual truth: and both adapted and transformed it instead of rejecting it. Its rejection was left for the next generation. Cézanne's pictures, painted just after he had broken away from the influence of Pissarro, and van Gogh's during his first few months in Arles, correspond exactly to the 'Good Shepherd' in Ravenna, and very nearly to the 'split' style of Duccio. They are new wine in bottles whose shapes are still, in essence, traditional.

The final rejection of the phase that began with Giotto and ended with Impressionism is evident enough to-day. It is not my purpose in this book either to account for modern art or to appraise it. My concern is with the particular problems of taste during a transitional period. For that a new chapter will be necessary.

CHAPTER X

Taste and Contemporary Art

I DOUBT IF THE INFLUENCE OF PHOTOGRAPHY ON PICTORIAL ART has been fully realised. Whenever, in the past, a machine has been invented to do what had hitherto been done by hand, there has been a momentary struggle followed by a sharp dividing of the ways. For, as writers on design in industry frequently point out, the hand can never work in the machine's way, and if the machine attempts to copy the hand, æsthetic disaster follows. None the less, during the brief struggle that follows the invention, the hand is invariably influenced by the feats of precision performed by the machine, and the machine, having no tradition of its own, invariably attempts to imitate the forms evolved by the hand.

Alberti, the founder of humanist æsthetics, was in no doubt as to the painter's aims. They were twofold. The first was to imitate Nature as closely as possible, and he actually refers to a reflection in a smooth surface—the reflection, for example, of Narcissus in the water—as a kind of ideal of this aspect of painting. The second was to make his work 'beautiful'. What Alberti meant by 'beauty' does not concern us here. But the method by which the two aims were to be reconciled—and evidently they were often bound to conflict with each other—was the simple one of painting from Nature, but always choosing the most beautiful things.

Leonardo, though more scientific in his approach than Alberti, held roughly the same view. Painting is superior to poetry because it "makes images of the works of Nature with more truth than the poet". Science can help the painter in making these images, but only because by science the painter can deduce laws which will save him the trouble of observing with the physical eye each object that he wishes to record. The intensity of the impact of light on any position of a sphere, given the amount and direction of the light, can be calculated. It need not be observed, *ab initio*, each time the artist wishes to paint a sphere.

If both these theorists on the art of painting had been told that four centuries after their deaths a machine would be invented which would automatically record shapes and intensities of light, they would have been puzzled and a little disconcerted. They would have felt, not so much that half the artist's occupation was gone as that the art of painting had been robbed of half its dignity and nobility. When the pedestrian was outstripped by the cyclist and the cyclist by the motorist, they could no longer afford to think in terms of speed. There were still many things to be said in favour of walking and cycling, but speed was not one of them. And after the invention of the camera it was still possible for the artist to make a Narcissus-reflection of Nature, but he could no longer boast about it. As a recorder he had been outstripped, and he could only console himself with the thought that recording was not everything, and concentrate on other tasks—among them the pursuit of 'beauty'.

There is little doubt that the invention of photography stimulated the Impressionists by presenting them with a record of the visible world that was in many ways different from that produced by any artist of the past. The world, as presented by the camera, was distinguished, not by a lack of clarity, but by a lack of emphasis. The camera's eye, unlike the artist's, was incapable of sorting the objects confronting it into categories—especially the categories of interesting and uninteresting, significant and insignificant. This objective view of life gave the photograph a curious and unfamiliar flavour which seemed to the Impressionist artist to have its own significance. It was, in fact, what he thought he was aiming at himself, and it helped certain artists—Degas in particular—to a new kind of composition which had all the appearance of objectiveness, but was in actual fact as calculated and personal as the more formal systems of composition of the past. Degas' habit of allowing his largest figures to collide with the frame and walk out of the picture is familiar enough. Monet's locomotive in his 'Gare St. Lazare' is half-way out of the picture. The effect is of having caught Nature on the move, but a fraction of a second too late to satisfy the accepted laws of composition. But since the laws of composition only exist in order to serve the needs of artistic expression, the truth is that, for the Impressionist, photography enlarged and modified the laws of composition.

The change was a temporary one. Much more fundamental was the subsequent change which took place as soon as the artist began to realise that his job as recorder, which I have described as the onion's outer skin, had been usurped by a mechanical device. Logically, there was nothing for him to do but to acknowledge that in his function of recorder he had been superseded, and to reconsider the whole purpose of pictorial art. He was in the position of a general who had suffered a major defeat, and who was therefore forced to retire and reconsider the whole theory of strategy and tactics.

In the arts it is sometimes necessary but always dangerous to theorise. Theorists tend to produce art that may be serious but can hardly be sensuous or human. But the beginning of the twentieth century was one of those moments in history when artistic theory was bound to flourish. The outer skin of the onion had become superfluous. Topographical landscape had become obsolete. Realism had become unnecessary. There was no reason why the painter should not, like Alberti, 'imitate Nature', but he could no longer boast about doing so. His problem evidently lay on another and a deeper level of the onion. And as the outer levels in general were too closely tied up to appearances, it seemed natural to start at the other extreme and see whether an æsthetic could be evolved which worked, as it were, from the centre outwards.

It was not an easy thing to do. I have already stressed the interdependence and the interpenetration of the levels in a work of art. But there is one aspect of their interdependence which has not hitherto been noted, namely that it operates in one direction only, from the outside inwards. Each level is conditioned by the one above it: each owes its meaning, and in fact its very existence, to the one above it.

At the risk of wearisome repetition, let me once more tabulate the onion's levels:

(1) Objective factual description of visible objects.
(2) Subjective comment on the objects described.
(3) Personal attitude to life in general.
(4) 'Beauty.'
(5) 'Handwriting.'

The progression advances, not only from the particular to the general, but also from the impersonal to the personal. At each advance towards the centre the artist approaches an experience which is not only more universal but is also more truly his own. But, oddly enough, he can only advance from the outside: he can only approach the general by way of the particular: he can only express the realms of emotion *after* experiencing the life of sensation.

It became evident, in my analysis of Veronese's picture, not only that each level melted imperceptibly into the next, but also that each level derived its full meaning from the one above it. Moreover, the whole onion depended for its potency on the soil in which it grew.

Unless Veronese had lived against a background in which the Catholic Church was strong enough to take the artist into its service to commission him to paint St. Catherine's mystical marriage, confident that the picture would convey its full literary meaning to a set of spectators who knew exactly what it stood for, it would never have been painted. Once the subject-matter has been dictated, Veronese has first of all to set his stage and people it with his characters, human and angelic. Until he has taken that first, purely objective step, he cannot begin to develop his personal comment on his characters or their environment. Again, it is only when he has made his comment on this particular event, and when we have compared this comment with other comments by him on other particular events, that we can deduce the personality, the generalised attitude underlying the comment. And not until this personality, this attitude of mind, has been established can he begin to evolve the æsthetic form which will be exactly appropriate to it. Finally, not until the æsthetic form has been imaginatively evolved can his 'handwriting'—the purely physical and material means by which it is made manifest—come into play. Handwriting is barren if there is no thought for it to express; thought is impossible unless there is a concrete stimulus to originate it; and the concrete stimulus can only come to the artist from the outside world in which he lives.

But though it is impossible to dispense altogether with the nourishing soil and the outer levels, it is certainly possible to minimise them and to concentrate on the inner ones. And that is what happened at the

Seurat, Le Chahut
Rijksmuseum Kröller-Muller, Otterlo, Holland

beginning of this century. Cézanne had a very definite attitude to the
visible world in general, though the particular set of visible objects he
happened to be painting held a minimum of interest for him. He was
not interested in his wife as a companion, as Rembrandt evidently was;

nor in apples as edible fruit, as Chardin certainly was. Both subjects seemed to him interesting only for their solidity and monumental possibilities. And both were interesting for precisely the same reason. His often-quoted remark about the ultimate reduction of all visible objects to a handful of geometric solids gives him away. An apple is to him not a fruit but an approximation to a sphere. So is his wife's head; and her arm is a tapering cylinder.

Seurat had equally definite theories about the psychological impact of certain kinds of line and composition, and though subject-matter was of considerable importance to him as providing a starting-point for an essay in composition, it had little intrinsic interest. The afternoon parade on the river-bank in 'La Grande Jatte' was a convenient *raison d'être* for a scheme of reposeful horizontals and static verticals; the high kick of the chorus girls in 'Le Chahut' provided him with an excuse for a set of urgent diagonals, and if the neck of the double bass in the foreground could manage to reinforce the diagonal lines of the girls' legs so much the better.

Van Gogh's interest in 'life' was more evident than Cézanne's or Seurat's (hence his greater popularity once the battle of Post-Impressionism was over), but it was largely by means of his 'handwriting' that he made it manifest. It is not handwriting for handwriting's sake, but it approaches as nearly to it as is safe without abandoning thought altogether. In the painterly transcriptions he made from the pictures of Delacroix and Millet, one sees exactly what qualities in the originals he was prepared to sacrifice in order to achieve the rhythmic vitality which plays so overwhelming a part in his painting.

Briefly, then, one can say that Cézanne thickened the third level, Seurat the fourth, van Gogh the second and fifth. All of them agreed in minimising the outer level. It was a risky proceeding, but none of them was to blame. If we are to discover the cause for the decay, in modern art, of the importance of subject-matter, it must be sought rather in the changed relationship between the artist and society than in any lack of normal humanity in the artist himself. But the equally striking decay of the importance of objective realism is certainly due, in part, to the invention of photography.

The fine arts, during the last 150 years, have suffered a double blow. First, society has ceased to *need* the painter of pictures in the same urgent

(*From* Escholier: *Delacroix, by permission of H. Floury, Paris*)

Delacroix, The Good Samaritan

sense in which it needs the designer of aeroplanes. Second, photography has robbed him of the obligation to make a record of appearances. Both these links with the outside world, the world of action, have been severed. The artist has therefore been driven to concentrate on the inner world, the world of contemplation, in which, it is true, he has always been a specialist, but which hitherto had always been nourished and invigorated by contact with the outer world.

Van Gogh, The Good Samaritan, after Delacroix

Rijksmuseum Kröller-Muller, Otterlo, Holland

These, then, were the first steps in the attempt to find an alternative to the Albertian theory of painting. They were naturally followed by bolder steps in all three directions. Cézanne's inhuman habit of dissection and analysis led, as historians of modern painting agree, to cubism: Seurat's emphasis on the purely architectural aspects of painting was bound to end in abstract art. Van Gogh's reliance on handwriting has led his successors to dwell more and more on the 'handling' of paint.

There is a limit to the amount of thickening or thinning that can be done to any given level, and the extreme limits of thickening of the inner levels and thinning of the outer levels that are characteristic of modern painting have probably now been reached. If this were a critical history of the experimental period in painting that started at the beginning of the twentieth century, it would be appropriate to define those limits. But I am concerned here with the attitude of the spectator and the reason why the art of the past fifty years has made special demands on his sensibilities. There never has been a period in which the consumer of art was so uncertain of his standards or when there was so much special pleading for and against the kind of painting I have briefly outlined above.

Most of that special pleading ignores the central fact that for the average spectator, too, the work of art can only be approached from the outside and that a thinning of the outer at the expense of the inner layers baffles him. Contemporary criticism is apt to regard these outer layers as a sugar coating to the essential artistic pill. Roger Fry has somewhere described subject-matter as a kind of bait which the artist uses to attract the spectator to his hook. Both images are, up to a point, correct, but they contain the absurd implication that sugar is undesirable and bait unnecessary. Such implications are essentially puritan, and since the normal consumer of art is not a puritan, one cannot expect him to be convinced by them.

Less and less—with the development of democracy, the spread of education, the increase of opportunity, through travelling exhibitions and multiplied reproductions, to become familiar with works of art—can the normal consumer be ignored. The curious situation in which art becomes more and more available to the average man—whose experience is most complete on the outer, the less abstract levels of painting, while the artist himself is concentrating more and more on the inner, the more purely æsthetic levels—must be faced. For in the process of facing it, the meaning of the word 'beauty' will surely emerge. At present the word becomes more difficult to use every day, yet the basic hunger for it persists, and even grows, as the opportunity for experiencing it grows.

The easiest way to face it will be to examine the normal *conservative* attitude to contemporary art, the attitude of the man who, accepting the Albertian theory of art ("truth plus beauty" as he would put it), is puzzled and distressed to find that a great many contemporary works of art seem to him both untrue and ugly, and that those very works of art are consistently praised by a small but far from negligible body of critics and art-lovers.

CHAPTER XI

Form and Content

"BUT WOULD YOU MARRY HER?" THE QUESTION, IN ALL ITS
simplicity, addressed to me about ten years ago by a middle-
aged artist about an unusually distorted painting of a figure—
just recognisably female—by Picasso, was uttered in anger; and the
anger, originally provoked by Picasso's ruthless reorganisation of the
human figure, had almost completely transferred itself, during the
course of a quarter of an hour's lively conversation in front of the
picture, from the picture itself to me. His chief causes of complaint
were my apparently inexplicable inability to dislike the picture because
of its distortion, and my equally inexplicable capacity to like it for
other reasons.

What makes the question memorable to me after so many years was
partly the concentrated fury behind it, but mainly the questioner's
conviction that it was unanswerable; that, after all other arguments
had been answered and all other rationalisations of his undeniably
sincere indignation had failed to convince me, here at least was a
question that I could not answer honestly without giving the game
away.

I think it was at that moment that I realised the reasonableness of
his question. It is a Philistine's question and therefore a superficial
question; the stock answers to it are easy—that the artist's business
is neither to copy Nature nor pursue the beautiful in Nature, but to
organise colour and form across the surface of the canvas, etc., etc.;
that the life of contemplation in which the arts have their being obeys
a different set of laws from the life of action in which alone words like
'marriage' have any meaning; that æsthetic beauty and human beauty
are only distantly related. But the stock answers are clichés. They are
just as superficial, in their way, as the Philistine's rhetorical question,

and though they are perfectly true they cannot be uttered with one-quarter of the passionate conviction that the Philistine puts into "But would you marry her?" Certainly Leon Battista Alberti, who was no Philistine, would have posed the same question as the Philistine of to-day. For Picasso had certainly done something in his picture which no European artist between the beginning of the fourteenth and the end of the nineteenth centuries would have thought of doing. He had ignored not merely the nobility but also the humanity of the human body. Even the impersonal Degas, even the cynical Toulouse Lautrec, implied the existence of a physical ideal by their very habit of pointing out that most women are not physically beautiful nor most men physically admirable. Even Gauguin's deliberate flight from Europe was merely a sign that he was exchanging one type of physical beauty for another. His protest was not against physical beauty *per se*, but against the narrow Hellenic version of it.

But Picasso's distortions are quite evidently neither a cynical comment on humanity nor an attempt to set up a new standard of human beauty. In order to find a parallel to them one has to go back to mediæval artists who had as little reverence for physical perfection as he, but for a different reason. To contemplate marriage with the female figures on a twelfth-century Provençal Romanesque façade or the thirteenth-century mosaic of Potiphar's wife in the atrium of St. Mark's in Venice would be as unthinkable as to marry one of Picasso's 'Demoiselles d'Avignon' painted in 1907. And though the modern Philistine would probably agree that this is true, he would do so with less passion and with little or no indignation.

It is high time that the Philistine was given his due. He is not wrong-headed; he is merely shallow. When he fails to grasp Picasso's meaning, he fails because, to adopt Roger Fry's analogy, Picasso refuses to bait the hook for him. And for that the angler is more to blame than the fish. It is vain to argue that the hook is what really matters and that the bait is irrelevant. Such an argument is only valid among the most puritan of angling circles. Among the fish down on the bed of the river it no longer holds good.

But Roger Fry's analogy is a bad one. It is based on the assumption that the producer and the consumer of art are two different species; that the one exists for the purpose of seducing the other; that it is somehow immoral to use any but the most honourable means of seduction; and that the only honourable means of artistic seduction are purely æsthetic.

Now, the purpose of this book is to attempt to isolate æsthetic beauty as a value, both in life and in art. And the result of the attempt has been to show that in life, beauty can only be defined as man's response to the mathematical behaviour of Nature, and in art, his expression and communication of that mathematical response in intensified form in terms of his given medium. In that sense the Picassian attempt to 'find' ("I do

Picasso, Les Demoiselles D'Avignon
Collection of the Museum of Modern Art, New York

(*Alinari photograph*)
Joseph and Potiphar's Wife. Detail from Mosaics in the
Atrium of St. Mark's, Venice

not seek, I find," is Picasso's own saying) beauty in life and to isolate
and intensify it in his painting is remarkably successful. To the
spectator who could entirely suppress his non-æsthetic appetites and
live a life in which association played no part, the Picassian system is
entirely satisfactory.

But such a spectator only exists in theory. *Homo æstheticus* is his
name, and he would perish within a few days if he ever occurred at all,
because he would have no appetites except for mathematical beauty.

The green meadow patterned with spots of white and yellow would be the same to him whether the spots were daisies and buttercups or torn paper and orange peel. He could dispose of the question, "But would you marry her?" by replying, quite honestly, "I am incapable of human love or human desire, therefore I have no wish to marry anyone. To me Picasso's woman is more mathematically exciting and therefore more satisfying than the rather uninteresting arrangement of pink forms known as the Rokeby Venus or the even less systematic arrangement of shape and colour known as the Mona Lisa."

It must be obvious that Æsthetic Man is just as incomplete as his counterpart, Philistine Man, and that a theory of beauty based on his limitations must be an unsatisfactory theory. It would, of course, be absurd to pretend that mathematical satisfaction by itself is valueless. Such an assertion would be equivalent to saying that the whole of æsthetic theory is invalid. Given the formal framework without which no work of art can exist, every element within the frame must be visually related to the frame itself and to every other element in the work of art. Without such established relationships acute visual discomfort would ensue. The eye would search in vain for the stability and balance on which every work of art depends and which criticism has agreed to call its formal value.

Every painting can easily be reduced to a set of basic mathematical terms, and at certain periods in the development of art this basic structure is as insistent in painting as it must always be in architecture. The mathematical devices used by the painter vary from age to age, but they are always devices, and their only object is to provide the stability and balance without which the spectator's demand for visual comfort would be defeated, so that the work of art within the frame becomes a formal unit obeying a set of visual laws that are just as rigid as the functional laws that govern the world outside the frame. The obvious device, used in a thousand altar-pieces of the fifteenth century, is the device of symmetry, and its commonest variant is the pyramid with a centre-line more or less specifically established. Pollaiuolo's 'Martyrdom of St. Sebastian' in the National Gallery is so extreme an example (in which the rigid symmetry of the isosceles triangle is pedantically filled with symmetrically disposed archers while the saint on his tree seems to have no other object than to provide a centre-line)

Pollaiuolo, Martyrdom of St. Sebastian
National Gallery, London

that the device becomes ludicrous; but some of Raphael's Madonnas, though far more subtly devised and varied, are equally rigid in construction.

Soon boredom with symmetry sets in. The centre-line is broken, the emphasis thrown to one side or the other and a new set of devices invented, but always in the interests of stability. Rubens's 'Deposition' has already been quoted as the apotheosis of the baroque diagonal. But the question I have been trying to answer throughout this book could be put somewhat like this. "Granted that the absence of this

Rubens, Portrait of Dr. Van Thulden
Pinakothek, Munich

mathematical basis to all the arts—and to painting in particular—
would be extremely unsatisfactory even to the Philistine and acutely
painful to the visually sensitive man, why make a fuss about it? It
exists even in mediocre paintings. In Pollaiuolo's altar-piece it is simple
and obvious: in Picasso's picture it is complex and subtle. But apart
from the negative fact that without it any painting would be intolerable, why is it so extremely valuable? If this is the secret of 'beauty',
it is surely too elementary a secret to account for the emotional power
of art over our conscious lives. Is *this* the reason why thousands of
pounds are willingly paid for works of art and millions of words have
been written in homage to genius and in explanation of its fascination?"

Of course it is not. The notion of form without content, or even of form divorced from content, is an untenable one; it is untenable as the notion of an Æsthetic Man without human appetites; yet it is a notion which seems to have an irresistible fascination for the critic and the 'abstract' artist. Even the elementary laws of form, stability, balance, and the interrelationships of part to whole, are in themselves a species of content. The very idea of stability is already half a literary idea. Pollaiuolo's vertical centre-line flanked by symmetrical diagonals is satisfying to the eye, not because it is functional and therefore inevitable. The laws of gravity compel us to feel that the vertical line—the path of the dropping apple, the axis of the growing tree or the standing man—has a particular significance; the supporting diagonals,

(Anderson photograph)

Bronzino, Portrait of Bartolomeo Panciatichi

Uffizi Gallery, Florence

like the stays of a ship's mast, increase the sense of steadiness. Only when an impression of a slight unsteadiness is required, as a protest against the immovable form so beloved of the fifteenth century, can a Titian break away from symmetry, and invent the formal asymmetry of the 'Pesaro Madonna'. That slight unsteadiness comes as a relief to the eye satiated with static forms. But in order to justify asymmetry a hundred little compensating subsidiary formal devices have to be introduced. Compare, for example, Bronzino's portrait of Panciatichi with Rubens's portrait of Dr. Van Thulden. The first, based on symmetry and on a vertical-horizontal system, is simple for all its Michelangelesque mannerisms. But for the rather unnatural agitation of the hands, it would be as rigid as a crossword puzzle. Even the axis of the sitter's head (placed exactly in the centre-line of the picture) is vertical, and the nose, one feels, has been artificially forced into a vertical in the interests of pure mathematics. (It is interesting, by the way, to note that close-up photographs of Michelangelo's 'Delphic Sibyl' in the Sistine Chapel, whose strength depends on the *absolute* vertical axis of her head, reveal the construction lines scored in the wet plaster. Not the outline of the head itself is marked, but the horizontal of the brows and the vertical of the nose; the lines are manifestly ruled with a set-square.) In Bronzino's portrait the architectural background contributes an unnecessary number of vertical lines. The unavoidable curve of the cap and the forehead have to be symmetrically reinforced by two arches introduced into the composition. Bronzino's geometry is archaistic. It derives from the classic formulæ of the late fifteenth century, and for that reason it is somewhat lacking in conviction. It has the air of an exercise in composition, and the psychology of the portrait has suffered in consequence.

How easily, on the other hand, does the diagonal sweep of Rubens's portrait seem to develop, not out of a determination to impose the baroque system of geometry on to the sitter, but out of a perfectly natural habit of mind which cannot help *seeing* a diagonal whenever a sitter settles himself comfortably into his chair. But note what new geometrical devices are involved in the new system. The moment it is put into practice, instability results. A diagonal line implies the intolerable notion of toppling over, and the expedient of introducing the kind of stays that keep the mast of a ship in position will no longer serve. That expedient depends on symmetry, and symmetry has been rejected, together with verticality. It is no longer the mast that needs supporting, but the whole ship. Dr. Van Thulden's head is no longer in the centre of the canvas, and its axis suggests no vertical line to relate it to the vertical edge of the painting. Left to itself, the whole figure will slide downwards and to the right—or rather the spectator's eye will slide. This asymmetry must be rectified and the heavy book (itself involved in the diagonal movement) and the hand that holds it do all that is necessary. A deep shadow in the left-hand bottom corner conceals the backward overhang of the whole mass and reduces the sense of 'toppling' to a minimum.

Now, the difference between the two portraits is not, fundamentally, the difference between two geometrical systems into which the image of a human being has been poured as a jelly is poured into a mould. It is rather the difference between two ways of looking at mankind. Both portraits are a species of metaphor. To say of a man that he is 'upright' is to express a psychological conception in geometrical terms. The form arises out of the content. It is itself a metaphor derived from the content. Both Bronzino and Rubens have discovered the appropriate visible equivalent of a state of mind, and if both portraits seem to obey laws of composition that are typical of the periods in which they were painted, that is because they express states of mind that were typical of their periods.

This, then, is the answer to my question about the mathematical basis to the arts. Its preciousness, to us, is not just a proof that mathematics provides us with a deep inner satisfaction, but that a state of mind, a whole philosophy of life, can, when a great artist is at work, discover its exact mathematical equivalent. It can become manifest as a set of purely formal relationships. Form and content are not two separate factors in a work of art which become separately more potent the more the form is appropriate to the content. They are actually different manifestations of the same factor. Content, for example, cannot be emptied out of form as wine can be emptied out of a bottle, by turning the picture upside down and thereby robbing it of its narrative or descriptive ingredients. Rubens's diagonal is something—the almost ultimate thing—without which he cannot say what he wants to say about Dr. Van Thulden. And even the features, the angle of the

189

brow, the line of the nose, the set of the chin, on which the 'likeness', the purely descriptive element in the portrait, depends—even these are caught up into the general rhythm of the picture. If a painter cannot manage to perform this miracle of turning concrete description into abstract form, he is a failure both as an artist and as a portrait painter. Even as a psychological document his portrait is weakened because the psychological message has not managed to find its exact formal equivalent. Everyone knows that wine cannot be drunk unless it is gathered conveniently into some kind of container. But the relationship is far closer than that. Unlike the wine and the bottle, the two cannot even be separated in thought. They are aspects of each other.

It is here that the Philistine's approach becomes inadequate. Looking at Picasso's picture—at its 'form', for that is all that his eyes can see—he translates it into purely descriptive terms. To him it is a representation of a woman, not an equivalent of a state of mind engendered by *that* woman, women in general, visual experience in general, colour, pattern, light, texture—the whole sum of a human being's sensations and perceptions. Hence his question, "Would you marry her?" The percentage of the picture that could reasonably be said to describe 'her' is negligible. And it so happens that Picasso has been at some pains to make it more negligible than it ever has been since the beginning of the Renaissance. The remaining percentage of the picture is the expression of a state of mind. One does not contemplate marriage with a state of mind.

To this the Philistine (let us credit him at least with a capacity for logical argument) will quote my own argument against me. "You have said that each level of a work of art derives its meaning from the one above it. Very well. Abide by the consequences of your own dictum. Here is a picture whose descriptive level is repulsive and disgusting, not only to me but to any sane person. Bronzino's portrait conjures up the image of a man I could admire: Rubens's Dr. Van Thulden I should find congenial: Picasso's picture, in so far as it is a description at all, describes a woman whom you as well as I would loathe. You taunt me with being unable to penetrate beyond this superficial level, but if each inner level ultimately derives its meaning from this outer level, this perversion of the visual truth, then even on your own admission the whole picture is tainted. To put it in the mildest terms, the picture is lacking in humanism in that it refuses to accept the human body as a standard. It is therefore ugly. If it is relevant to say, as many serious critics have said of Michelangelo's Sistine Chapel Adam, 'A magnificent conception of a man,' then it is equally relevant to say of this painting 'A disgusting conception of a woman'."

I have stated the Philistine's case as strongly as I can, and it is a difficult case to answer as long as humanism is the dominant and accepted creed. But the Philistine will do well to remember that humanism has by no means always been the accepted creed. "Man is the measure of all things" was the creed of the pre-Christian Hellenic culture, and again of the Renaissance culture, which, as I see it, is at last moribund, after dominating the whole of Europe for six centuries. But those two periods do not comprise the whole history of civilisation, and wherever and whenever man has regarded his gods as all-powerful, and life as a mystery beyond his control, art has not been humanistic and human 'beauty' has not been the standard.

Chinese art, Mexican, African, Mediæval European art were not primarily concerned with man in his earthly environment. Therefore their artists were under no obligation to *love* man and his environment in their hearts, nor to praise and ennoble them in their works. Only because the Philistine demands that they should do so does he regard their works as ugly and incomprehensible. But it is noteworthy that once direct references to man have been left behind, even the Philistine can see beauty. An African mask or carved human figure or an Aztec god is ugly because non-humanist, but a ceremonial canoe paddle or a carved beaker is beautiful. The very detachment which makes a Chinese figure seem remote and soulless, or a Romanesque saint impossibly incorporeal, makes a Chinese vase exquisite and a mediæval chalice beautiful. The curves, the rhythms, may be the same in both, but the outer skin of description in the first is impenetrable to the Philistine. The second he accepts gladly because it has no outer skin.

"Impenetrable" is, perhaps, too strong a word. The Philistine is almost always sufficiently far-seeing to penetrate beyond the purely descriptive layer to the superficial emotive layers immediately below it. It needs little enough penetration, for example, to see in the girl on the magazine cover, not only a representation of a human being, but a symbol of sex-appeal, though the Philistine is not always aware that these two aspects of the same work of art are separable. In an earlier chapter I quoted the critic of the *Literary Gazette* who, in 1830, said of James Ward's 'Venus rising from her Couch': "It is badly drawn, badly coloured, and what is much worse, indelicate. Why are the modest and lovely young females who daily grace the rooms of Somerset House with their presence to have their feelings outraged and blushes called into their cheeks by a work like this?"

Quite apart from the fact that the critic has contradicted himself— it requires good or at least adequate drawing and colouring to convey sex-appeal strongly enough to arouse a blush—it is evident that having penetrated to the picture's second level, the critic has stuck there. His experience of sex is complete enough and (since he is living in the heart of a romantic period) exaggerated enough to enable him to judge the picture as a sex-stimulant, and to be indignant at its power as such —indignant, be it noted, not on his own behalf, but on behalf of modest young females (and, oddly enough, lovely young females) who, it might have been expected, would have been less prone to such stimulation than himself. It is odd, too, that the critic of Picasso's picture was indignant for almost exactly the opposite reason. Picasso's lady lacks the sex-appeal that would bring her an offer of marriage. The Philistine, it seems, is rather difficult to please.

The critic of 1830 has not succeeded in penetrating beyond this elementary level. Or, if he has, he has omitted to say so. Considering that ever since the last quarter of the fifteenth century the naked human body has been one of the painter's major concerns, one would have expected him to explain why James Ward was more capable of arousing blushes than Correggio or Rubens or his own contemporary, Ingres.

Doubtless, if pressed, he would attempt to do so, but his explanations would probably be unconvincing, and he certainly would not be frank enough to admit the real cause of his failure—namely, his lack of understanding which in its turn is based on his lack of experience.

Certain fields of experience are so universal that it is rare to find an adult human being who has not accumulated a rich store of them. They are the fields of experience which are of biological use to him. It is inevitable that, in general, the average man should collect a formidable stock of visual memories connected with the edibility of food, the desirability of women, the state of mind of a friend; and that even the

simplest forms of specialisation make these kind of experiences acute
and intense. The cyclist can judge the gradient of a road, the farmer
the condition of a crop, the dressmaker the quality of a textile to a
nicety, because so much depends on their capacity to judge. But in
fields where experience is not biologically useful, the stimulus to
accumulate it is lacking and the average man's stock of it is lamentably
meagre.

Now art is no more than the expression of human experience; and
the understanding and enjoyment of art is no more than the capacity
of the spectator to relate the work of art to his own accumulated store
of experience. It follows that the spectator's reaction to the work of
art is limited by the scope of his experience. The Philistine is not wrong-
headed when he complains that James Ward is too sexually stimulating
for his comfort, or Picasso too little. He—in common with most
adults—is a good judge of such matters. He is working entirely by
association. No sooner does he see a picture by Ward or Picasso than
he refers what he has seen to his own accumulated memories of women,
and they in their turn bring a hundred associated trains of thought with
them. He is perfectly right when he says that Ward is inconveniently
stimulating *on this level*, and Picasso disgustingly unstimulating. His
limitation—what marks him out as a Philistine—is that his associations are almost entirely confined to the realm of the biologically useful.
To laugh at him for being mistaken would be absurd and unjust.
Certainly he is to be pitied for his narrowness. But Æsthetic Man,
who refuses to find any sexual associations—or is incapable of finding
them—in the two paintings, is even more to be pitied. *His* narrowness
is even more remarkable. Moreover, if, as usually happens, it is a pose,
it is worse than narrow: it is insincere.

It is appropriate at this point to make a short but important digression into the realms of style, and to remember that the whole weight
of European tradition has been built up, since the beginning of the
Renaissance, on the assumption that the painter must cover the whole
surface of his picture with descriptive matter. I am not referring to the
theory of realism, but to the more fundamental theory that the whole
of his picture must have a descriptive *meaning*. This theory has bitten
so deep into the consciousness of every European that we have ceased
to think of it as extraordinary or even interesting. We have ceased to

Chinese Still Life, Bamboo Shoots
From the Eumorfopoulos Collection, British Museum

realise it at all. And yet it has by no means always been accepted by other civilisations. An area of blue paint in the upper part of a landscape by Constable *means* a cloudless sky. An area of green paint in the background of a still life by Picasso *means* a green wall. However distorted the forms in the picture may be, the very fact that one can use the word 'background' shows that one sees the picture as a representation of objects in space, and that Picasso, though he has outgrown the Renaissance view of life, has not, for all his revolutionary courage, abandoned the Renaissance theory of painting.

One has only to remember that a plain sky in a Chinese landscape is *not* intended to indicate an absence of clouds but only a refusal to make any statement about clouds, and that the area of silk or paper 'behind' a Chinese still life is *not* in any sense a representation of a featureless background, in order to realise that the Renaissance theory that every square inch of a painting must convey visual information is certainly not a universally accepted theory. The European picture, however stylised or distorted, is always basically a representation: the Chinese picture is a self-contained symbol. The same is true of mediæval European art. Visual information, even about forms that exist only in the artist's imagination, is not part of its intention. Renaissance art has no alternative but to accept that intention; and the average adult European to-day is forced, by the tradition in which he grew up, to make the same set of assumptions when he looks at a painting.

The distinction between the two theories of art may seem at first sight a trifle academic, but a good many practical results follow from it. There is an assumption, for instance, that a painting in which the whole surface is not covered with paint is somehow 'unfinished'.

(*Courtesy of Louis Carré Gallery, Paris*)

Picasso, Still Life, March 14, 1945

Even more fundamental is the *kind* of association evoked in the spectator's mind by the two types of art. The apocryphal legends that have grown up round them make this quite clear. The type of European legend is of the grapes that were so convincingly painted that the birds pecked them. The type of Asiatic legend is of the painted dragon which the artist refused to supply with eyes lest it should fly away. The difference is between a representation and a thing-in-its-own-right. And the question "Would you marry her?" could only be asked by a spectator brought up on the grapes-and-birds theory. The Chinese painted dragon was not to be judged by its resemblance to a dragon but by its capacity to *be* a dragon.

That does not mean that the Chinese work of art is less closely related to life than the European; its relationship is equally close, but it is a different kind of relationship. Every artist, whether he is producing a symbol or a representation, nourishes himself on his visual experience. Before he can paint a man or a mountain, either realistically or symbolically, he must have seen and experienced a man or a mountain. Every spectator, too, before he can judge the painting, must have had a similar experience, and must relate the work to his experience and enjoy it by virtue of that relationship. But again, for him, the relationship is different according to whether he is looking at a representation or a symbol. For a representation, however idealised, always carries with it a suggestion of the particular case; and a symbol, however specific, must always suggest the universal, the grapeness behind the grape, the femininity behind the woman. Hence the relevant question would be not "Would you marry her?" but "Does it (not 'she') enlarge or disturb your conception of womanhood?"

It is a more serious question, but it deprives the Philistine of his chief pleasure, the pleasure of clinging to the specific, the material world, and it forces him to move in the, to him, unfamiliar world of abstract thought and emotion. Whenever he is confronted with this world through contact with the art of another age or an alien culture, he can to some extent avoid the issue by calling it 'archaic' or 'decorative'. But whenever he meets it in contemporary guise he is baffled and disturbed. The effort of seeing the work of art as anything but either a bad representation of a familiar object or a good representation of an undesirable object is too much for him. He cannot penetrate to the artist's ultimate intention, and the Renaissance theory of representation in art adds to his difficulty.

The artist's total intention certainly includes the field of biologically useful experience which the Philistine can easily share with him, but it goes far beyond that into regions denied to the Philistine. And it is only in these regions that Rubens and Titian begin to have any advantage over James Ward and Etty. The critic of the *Literary Gazette*, if he had been capable of exploring these regions, could still have made the same comment on the propriety of Ward's picture. And in view of the moral code of his decade, he would have been a hypocrite not to do so. For a picture of an object is, among its other functions, a reminder of the real object, and thereby acquires the same associations as the object. And if the moral code of the period considers these associations undesirable, the critic is justified in saying so. But he is not justified in saying nothing else. While he was writing, Rubens's 'Judgment of Paris', Correggio's 'School of Love', Bronzino's 'Venus, Cupid, Folly and Time' were hanging unreproved in the National Gallery, and it was his duty to speak out, to include them in his general displeasure or else to explain why he made exceptions in their favour.

Now it is rightly and universally assumed that the girl on the magazine cover belongs to a lower category of artefacts than Rubens's 'Judgment of Paris'. But there is only one reason that makes it so— its inability to evoke more than one set of associations. That it can at least do that—and do it effectively—is a virtue. But it is a virtue that it shares with Rubens's picture, and as soon as one realises how many, how varied, and how profound are the associations that Rubens can evoke, the limitations of the magazine cover are at once seen in all their one-sided triviality. It is not that there is "more to look at" in the Rubens—trees, clouds, sunlit distances, an animated foreground—it is that Rubens has brought a more universal mind to bear on each element in his picture so that only a receptive mind of similar universality can enjoy it to the full, though there is plenty in it, on the magazine-cover level, that the Philistine can enjoy too.

"To the full" is a phrase with massive implications. In theory only the creator of a given work of art can enjoy it to the full, for only he knows the exact shades of thought and emotion that are contained within it—that, in the most literal of senses, 'inform' it. But he, the creator, is a bad enjoyer of works of art in general. By the very intensity of his own thought and emotion, he is blinded to the thought and emotion of other artists. He is, by definition, a man of narrow but intense sympathies. History is full of instances of great artists who failed to realise the greatness of their own contemporaries. It is the man of wide experience, the cultured man, who is most capable of enjoying art "to the full". Genius can take wing from any stratum of society, but for the understanding of genius a full life—including what is known as education—is necessary. And it is precisely education in the richest sense of the word that enables men to acquire those kinds of experience which are biologically *unnecessary* but æsthetically indispensable.

For the full enjoyment of the girl on the magazine cover, it is only necessary to have experienced the elementary and normal stimulus of sex in its simplest form. But for the full enjoyment of Rubens it is necessary to have known, in addition, the vigour of trees, the pride of the peacock, the ordered tumult of the sky, the serenity of light falling on distant fields, the lushness of grass and the hardness of rock and, above all, the restless complexity and abundance of material life. And even these—which Rubens, of all artists, commands with such magnificence —are superficial experiences compared with the more elusive emotional levels that art can reach. The artists who can reach them are not necessarily the difficult or unpopular artists, though sometimes they have been so. Piero della Francesca is the type of painter who—because of that breathless, unearthly tension in which all the sensuous and vigorous joy of life has been dissolved away, leaving a kind of visual silence, an empty expectancy—can never be popular. But that is not because he penetrates too deeply and demands too much; it is because for all his penetration he cannot include the crude raw material of humanism so easily available to a Titian and Rubens. They can appeal to familiar human appetites and take the girl on the magazine cover, as it were, in their stride. Piero cannot, and because he cannot he is a smaller man. But the greatest creative artists are equally evocative on every level, and for that reason they are unlike the Pieros and Botticellis and el Grecos, who are forgotten by the generations that cannot understand them and over-praised by those that can. They are potent in every age, but potent to each for a different reason. And they are potent to every class, but potent to each on a different level.

For this reason in analysing the deeper and more elusive levels of beauty, it is the less universal artist who provides the best laboratory specimen, for in his case there is no need to ask, "Am I being seduced by what is crude and easy in his work?" Knowing that he is never quite human enough to be crude and easy, we know that we are in no danger of seduction. The pride of the peacock, the lushness of grass and the tumult of the sky have no place in the art of Piero and his kind.

Now, it is easy and it is true to say of such artists that they are lacking in response to the pageantry of the world; but that negative statement does not explain them. At the present moment Piero is at the height of his fame. We respond to his rarefied magic as no previous generation has done. It is not entirely his quietude that attracts us, for the very same persons who respond to the tranquillity of Piero succumb also to the violence of Picasso. It is not the mood itself that counts but the quality of it, and in particular its *distance* from the original visual experience which was its starting-point.

How is one to measure this emotional distance? Even to conceive it as measurable is not easy. Yet it is an essential concept in the analysis of beauty. A Nativity by Rubens, one feels intuitively (and therefore one knows), is nearer to the life of action than a Nativity by Piero. Not that it contains more action, but that it abounds in specific references— *this* fold of flesh, *this* jewel, *this* lock of hair with this particular direction and intensity of light falling on it. It is nearer to the surface of experience, and therefore it will be enjoyed by a generation that lives near to the surface.

But Piero, who had, we can assume, normal eyesight, and who, as he looked about him, *saw* this jewel, this fold of flesh, refuses to pass them on to us in his picture until they have sunk deep down into his consciousness. They have left the life of action far behind, and have become part of the life of contemplation wherein each object ceases to be specific and becomes generic. The apple, the tree trunk, cease to be *this* apple, *this* tree trunk; they even cease, with the process of emotional digestion, to be very apple-like or tree-like. They move into a remoter world, in which the apple loses its identity in its parent the sphere and the tree trunk is merged in the cylinder. This remotest of worlds, the world of mathematics, cold, orderly, inhuman yet magical, is the ultimate goal of every artist; every artist is compelled to make the perilous journey towards it from his starting-point in the world of the senses. And for every artist there is a point on the journey beyond which he dare not go for fear of losing touch with the lovable muddle of the sensual world. How far he may leave the apple behind, how near he may approach to the sphere without losing his delight in the specific apple, to what degree he can leave the warm muddle behind in his journey to the ultimate world of perfect order and harmony, is a problem which each artist has to work out for himself. And, if in working it out he finds himself too rigidly involved in this geometrical world, he will also find to his cost that it will refuse to contain certain levels of his experience. The set of forms and rhythms, for example, evolved by the Cubists are incapable of containing the kind of experience that was so precious to Rubens. Certainly they were deliberately evolved because they were the ideal means of saying what the Cubists were particularly anxious to say; but they take the artist so far on the journey towards the world of formal harmony that he finds himself cut off from the world of sensuous experience. The Cubists themselves realised this, and have since retired to a safer position; they had sacrificed too much. Their chosen means of expression was admirable in many ways: it was even inevitable. But there were too many levels of experience which it was incapable of expressing.

The artist, faced with this eternal problem, knows that he must make *some* sacrifice in the interests of formal design; his solution of it depends on the sacrifice he is prepared to make, and his sacrifice takes its value from the intensity of his love of life.

It is impossible for Rubens, it is easy for Mondrian and the abstract painters, to travel the whole distance, for they are prepared to jettison the whole of the visible world—peacocks, clouds, women and flowers—on their journey to their mathematical destination. They do not love life enough to regret that they travel light and arrive empty-handed, so that their spheres have lost all the sensuous implications of the apple and their cylinders have none of the strength of the tree. They are heartless theorists, who do not know that it is not arrival but the journey that counts. The sacrifice they have made is no sacrifice at all, for they have persuaded themselves that what they left behind them was valueless. To enjoy their work to the full may be difficult for the Philistine with his heavy burden of everyday associations, but for the æsthete who, like them, travels light, it is easy—as easy as it is to enjoy a fleshless skeleton to the full.

What, then, *is* this delight in mathematics which the purist constantly points to as the root of beauty? Plato, groping, as so many philosophers have groped, for a formula which would isolate absolute as opposed to relative beauty, decided that the only forms which are beautiful *in their own right* are "straight lines and curves and the surfaces or solid forms produced by lathes and rulers and squares". These, he says, "have their proper pleasures not depending on the itch of desire".

The theory is superficially attractive, but it smacks of wishful thinking. It is difficult to abandon the search for a yardstick, an absolute. And it is natural that the philosopher who insists on looking for a yardstick should search for it, not among the shifting forms of organic life, but in the rigid world of mathematics where the centre of the circle is *always* equidistant from every point on the circumference. The pleasure of contemplating these forms is, says Plato, untainted by "the itch of desire".

I doubt whether it is possible, philosophically speaking, to think of pleasure as anything but the sensation that results from gratified desire. Without appetite, without the discomfort of hunger, how can pleasure exist at all? And if Plato will contradict himself and grant me that there *is* a basic desire to contemplate mathematical relationships, and that the only purely æsthetic pleasure consists in such contemplation, I still ask him to explain whence came this desire. And if he replies that the world is unintelligible unless we can grasp the relationships between its parts —the relationship (which the eye alone can assess) between the centre of the circle and its circumference, or between the various sections of a line whereby we can judge whether it is straight or curved—and that in so far as a chaotic world is unintelligible and therefore intolerable, then an ordered, law-abiding, mathematical world, being the opposite of intolerable, is therefore delightful in its own right and not by association; if that is his reply, I can only answer that the delight of contemplating a circle is not basically different from the delight of contemplating a man. It differs enormously in degree: its mathematical formula is easier to divine: it satisfies one hunger instead of many: it is comparatively (though not quite) free from associations: like a man it is symmetrical, but unlike a man it cannot speak. Therefore it can satisfy a craving for visual orderliness, but for no other kind of orderliness. But even that satisfaction is, I believe, a satisfaction through association. The work of art that restricts itself to pure mathematics is pleasurable because it reminds us of the pleasures of orderliness and stability. It is only 'pure' in the sense that its associations are reduced to a minimum. The notion that somewhere there exists a pure æsthetic, divorced from life, a world that satisfies an innate hunger of the eye and needs no confirmation from the mind or the memory, is surely untenable. The true function of the underlying mathematical form in a work of art is at once more explicable and more mysterious.

What finally counts in the weight of beauty that a given work of art can sustain is its capacity to bear the burden of human experience, as a skeleton, meagre in itself, can sustain muscles and nerves, vital organs and skin.

We look at the painting and see nothing but its form, for there is nothing else to see. We listen to the poem read aloud and hear nothing but a voice. Presently the eye, resting on that area of line and colour, the ear reacting to that succession of syllables, begin to divine a rhythm, a mathematical pulse beating in space or time. What the artist created we begin to re-create, relating it, in time, to the beating of our own hearts, the echo of our own footsteps; in space, to the proportions of our own bodies, the pattern of the flowered meadow, the upward thrust of the pine tree, the level line of the horizon.

No sooner does the eye or the ear begin its exploration of this mathematical world of sight and sound than a meaning begins to emerge. Slowly the skeleton assumes the fleshly garment without which it is valueless. The rhythm of the poem and the rhythm of the human heart, the rhythm of the picture and the rhythm of the pine tree, become connected in the spectator's mind, and through that connection he knows that another human being is speaking to him, and that *his* ear, too, heard the beating of a heart, and *his* eye, too, knew the vertical stem of the tree. The process of association, the linking up of two sets of human experience, has begun—the recognition that life itself has given rise in the artist to a contemplative excitement, and that the excitement has been canalised and ordered into forms and sounds whose relationship to each other can be grasped and enjoyed by the spectator or the listener.

Presently the stream of associations thickens; the recognition of this elemental rhythmic life gives place to a recognition of its specific mood. Tranquillity or exuberance, joy or despair, suavity, violence, laughter are caught in the net of beauty, and they in their turn become more specific as the associations pour in. Not merely joy but the joy of health, not suavity alone but the suavity of a summer afternoon, until at last, if the artist is capable of beckoning and we are understanding enough to follow, we find ourselves by his side with the specific case, the fully clothed skeleton, between us.

This *was* the marriage of St. Catherine with the Infant Jesus, thus did Bacchus spring from his car to embrace Ariadne, here is God in the act of creating Adam, and Philip IV standing moodily by his table in the palace; and here is a loaf of bread and a jug of wine.

Does it matter whether these are the dreams of the Pagan or the symbols of the Christian world; the prosaic appearance of a Spanish king or the contents of a kitchen table? Certainly those are the stories they tell, but they are of no more (and no less) significance than the complexion of the skin. If they are to become nets to ensnare beauty, we must make the journey to the very core of them, taking with us, at each stage in the journey, all the accumulated associations which, in the fullness of life, we have gathered. At last we reach again the primeval world of the beating heart and the growing tree, and penetrate through it to the pure world of abstract form which *is* the picture.

Will that abstract world contain the burden we have collected? Will the skeleton support the flesh, will the net contain the catch? If so, then the work of art, because of its powers of containing and our powers of collecting, will be beautiful.

CHAPTER XII

Definitions

T HE ONLY ADVANTAGE OF DEFINITIONS IS TO CONVINCE THE writer of them that his conclusions are neither illogical nor, within their limitations, incomplete. A definition sheds no light on what is defined; it merely isolates it.

The following definitions are therefore no concern of the reader. I include them merely as a sign that I am satisfied that the conclusions arrived at in this book are valid so far as they go. That they do not go very far, no one is more conscious than myself.

Beauty is that aspect of phenomena which, when perceived by the senses and thence referred to the contemplative faculty of the perceiver, has the power to evoke responses drawn from his accumulated experience.

The test, in any given case, of its presence and intensity is a sensation of pleasure in the perceiver caused by the gratification of his desire to repeat his experience on a contemplative level; such desire is itself generated by experience on any level.

Therefore the richer the experience of the beholder and the greater his capacity for contemplation, the more complete his equipment for perceiving beauty—the 'better', as the phrase goes, his 'taste'.

Form and content in art are indivisible. They belong to different categories, and cannot be thought of as divisible, since they cannot be thought of as united. The only way of expressing their relationship is to say that one is an aspect of the other.

Form is content expressed in mathematically measurable terms.

Content is the sum of human experience for which the artist can discover a formal equivalent in his work of art.

All human experience can be expressed in terms of love or hate. Love is the creative, hate the destructive, agency. Both are necessary. To plant the lily and eradicate the weed are both necessary functions of the gardener.

Nature has no content, since her form is not an equivalent of human experience. The form of Nature is function expressed in mathematically measurable terms.

The only love one can detect in Nature is a love of efficiency.

Function creates form. Only when form is contemplated (i.e. is perceived purged of all ideas of function) can it be thought of as beautiful. The desire to drink blinds one to the beauty of the cup: the beauty of the cup interferes with the desire to drink. Yet the cup is a product of thirst.

Veronese, The Mystical Marriage of St. Catherine

Accademia, Venice